# History of Firefighting in New Bern North Carolina

# Colonial Days to the 21ˢᵗ Century

---

**Daniel Bartholf**

Cover design by Eugene Gibson, Copy & Print Warehouse, New Bern

On the Front Cover: (Top) Five steamers pumping from the Neuse River at the 1895 North Carolina Firemen's Convention and Tournament in New Bern.  **Photo from the New Bern Firemen's Museum Collection**

(Bottom)  1950s picture of New Bern Fire Department.  *From the New Bern Firemen's Museum Collection*.

On the Back Cover: (Top) *New Bernian* newspaper December 2, 1922

(Bottom) Amoskeag steamer in front of Broad Street station.  *Courtesy of the State Archives of North Carolina*

**Copyright ©2019 Daniel P. Bartholf    All rights reserved.**

History of Firefighting in New Bern NC – Colonial Days to the 21st Century

# Table of Contents

| | |
|---|---|
| Acknowledgements | 4 |
| Introduction | 5 |
| Chapter 1 Colonial Times Thru 1861 | 7 |
| Chapter 2 Civil War Years | 18 |
| Chapter 3 Post Civil War to 1900 | 25 |
| Chapter 4 Black Fire Companies | 46 |
| Chapter 5 Other Independent Fire Companies | 52 |
| Chapter 6 Notable Chief Engineers of the 19th Century | 55 |
| Chapter 7 Early 1900s | 60 |
| Chapter 8 The Great Fire December 1, 1922 | 85 |
| Chapter 9 1923-1959 | 104 |
| Chapter 10 1960-1999 | 114 |
| Chapter 11 2000-Present | 131 |
| Chapter 12 Competition 1880s-early 20th Century | 136 |
| Chapter 13 The Horses | 162 |
| Chapter 14 The Mystery of the Missing Fire Truck | 165 |
| Chapter 15 New Bern Firemen's Museum | 168 |
| Appendix A   History of New Bern fire companies | 176 |
| Appendix B   Chief Engineers of New Bern Fire Dept. 1800s | 177 |
| Appendix C   Chiefs of New Bern Fire Dept 1900-Present | 178 |
| Appendic D   A Snapshot in Time of the Department | 180 |
| Appendix E   1875 New Bern Steam Engine | 184 |
| Appendix F   Roster of 1828 Fire Companies | 189 |
| Appendix G   Fire Stations | 192 |
| Appendix H   Fire Apparatus | 202 |
| Appendix I   Notification of Fire | 221 |
| Map of Fires Set by Confederates Fleeing the City in 1862 | 229 |
| Map of New Bern | 230 |
| About The Author | 231 |

# Acknowledgements

I would like to recognize the following for their assistance in researching material and providing historical background information that made this book possible:

**Mike Legeros**, noted historian of the Raleigh Fire Department, who has provided an extensive amount of information on the history of North Carolina fire departments on his website: legeros.com.

**John B. Green III** from the New Bern Craven County Library

**Jim Hodges**, Curator, New Bern Historical Society

**Sarah Carrier**, Research & Instructional Services Department, Louis Round Wilson Special Collections Library, The University of North Carolina at Chapel Hill, Wilson Library

**William H. Brown**, Registrar, North Carolina Division of Archives and Records

**Kim Andersen and Vann Evans,** Audiovisual Materials Archivists, Special Collections, Archives of North Carolina

**Edward P. Brinson**, Deputy Director, North Carolina State Firemen's Association

My friends at the New Bern Firemen's Museum who provided support and historical information

**Chief Robert Boyd, Jr., Henry Watson,** and Past Chief and long-time member of the New Bern Fire Department, **Albert Brinson (member since 1957).**

**Brenda E. Blanco**, New Bern City Clerk

My son **Andrew** for his interest in helping with the research

**Robert Maloney** at *Fire Engineering* magazine.

**Gary R. Urbanowicz**, Executive Director, NYC Fire Museum

Thank-you to **Dolores Sauerwald** for editing the manuscript.

# Introduction

When I became a tour guide with the New Bern Firemen's Museum in 2017, I had no idea I would write a book about the firefighting history in this city. As I dug through what accounts there were, I became intrigued by the unique nature of the fire companies and the influence of, for instance, New York City during the Civil War, the segregated city and independent companies, and the evolution from the first hand pumper to the present-day department. There were portions of the history that seemed to be missing which would require an in-depth look at old newspaper accounts and city records which date back to the 1700s. Some city records are missing, but fortunately there were several newspapers in town through the 1800s and early 1900s. Newspapers were accessed for the most part via the website newspapers.com.

I've chosen to write the history with a timeline of significant events interspersed with the narration to better show the evolution of the formation of the fire companies and the difficulties inherent in the early years. Notes from the aldermen meetings are also included in this style to give you an idea of the inner workings of government. In addition, the bidding process is shown for the purchases of various pieces of apparatus to give the readers insight into this process and to show the astronomical increase in the costs over the years.

All estimated losses from fire are in the dollars of the particular time. To reflect the amounts in today's dollars, you would have to multiply the amount in 1860 by 30, in 1890 by 27, and the amount in 1920 by 12.

A note about the spelling of New Bern through history. In 1723 the General Assembly designated that the place be known as New Bern. Over time, many ways of spelling the town emerged including Newbern, New Berne, and Newberne. The 1793 General Assembly spelled the name as Newbern in its official publications. In 1897 the General Assembly revisited the topic and proclaimed that New Bern was the proper name. But don't look at the 1914 American LaFrance engine in the department…. it's spelled New Berne!

# Chapter 1

## Early Firefighting-Colonial Days to mid-1800s

"No Burn"   Photo: Andrew Bartholf

Located at the confluence of the Neuse and Trent Rivers in eastern North Carolina, New Bern is home to a rich firefighting history dating back to colonial times. Founded in 1710 by Christopher deGraffenried of Berne, Switzerland, New Bern is the second oldest city in North Carolina (Bath was incorporated in 1705), once served as the provincial capital in 1766 and briefly served as the state capital. The city adopted the armorial bearings and colors of Berne, Switzerland, and most notably the Swiss bear (Bern is the Swiss word for bear) depicted on the city's crest, displays and monuments around town.

As with many cities and towns during the early years, firefighting took a back seat to many other functions. Fires were not all that common, but when a large fire occurred, interest would grow in forming a fire company or brigade. But as time wore on the cities **would** drift back into an apathy until the cycle was repeated. New Bern was no exception to this.

In searching through the records and newspapers of the time in New Bern, there is no evidence of any organized fire company or equipment except for leather buckets and ladders until late in the eighteenth century. This despite the fact that New Bern was a rapidly growing port city.

Trying to identify when an organized fire company was present in a city in these early years is difficult. For example, Wilmington acquired the first hand pumper in North Carolina in 1756, a rig made in England. The city hired a caretaker to maintain and routinely operate the pumper. Several caretakers did not do their job, and the pumper fell into disrepair. A second hand pumper was purchased in 1773 from an American company to replace the first one. In neither case was a fire company organized to operate the pumpers. It's unclear when the first firefighting force was organized there but we know it may have been comprised of slaves. (*Lower Cape Fear Historical Society, Inc. Bulletin*, Vol. XVIII, Number 3, May 1975)

The first reference to firefighting in legislation was Chapter XIX of the Acts of the North Carolina General Assembly in 1773 which gave permission to New Bern for the purchase of a fire engine and upon its arrival a fire company would be appointed. It also specified that homes would have two leather water buckets and a ladder at least 25 feet long for fighting fire.

A fire in 1791 that began near the corner of Craven and South Front Streets destroyed 160 homes and businesses, about a third of the city. An article in the November 11, 1791 *Star Gazette of North Carolina* concerning a large fire in New York City that was rapidly brought under control by their numerous fire engines referred to New Bern's 1791 fire:

> "It is more than probable, had an institution of this kind existed in
>
> the town of Newbern, North Carolina, when 160 houses were reduced
>
> to cinders... that not more than two or three buildings would have fell
>
> sacrifice, nor more than one family to forty have been reduced to that
>
> kind of distress..."

Other large fires occurred on October 25, 1794, which leveled nine buildings in the center of town on Craven Street, and one on November 17, 1794 which destroyed 24 buildings including the New Berne Academy.

New Bern did not purchase a fire engine for at least 20 years after the authorization. Part of the delay is most likely related to the Revolutionary War. The first reference to a "water" engine was in 1794. And then, only a caretaker was assigned to routinely exercise the engine and respond to any alarms of fire. There was a fire watch in town whose duty was to detect fires and lawlessness, and upon discovering fire, to ring the church bell, inform the person who had care of the engine, and to alert citizens nearest the fire to the danger and ask them to assist in quelling the fire. (Dec. 6, 1794 The North Carolina Gazette)

In September 1797, the town started an inspection program for chimneys and began enforcing the rules for turpentine distilleries. Distilleries had to be located outside the city's limits. Baker's ovens had to be located away from combustible materials.

The Tryon Palace, once home to the colonial governor, but by the late 1700s in a state of disrepair, burned in February 1798. There is little evidence to support the idea that there was an organized fire company. The militia and citizens tried to control the fire by breaching hallways that connected the buildings on the grounds, but to no avail. Only the stables and kitchen remained standing after the fire. After this fire, another fire engine was ordered.

William Tignor was appointed on November 20, 1798 to keep the two fire engines in proper order. He also washed and examined them at least once a month. For this he was paid 6 pounds per year. Six fire hooks and 35 leather buckets were purchased.

A regulation in 1798 from the General Assembly of the state of North Carolina authorized and required that the town of Newbern form fire companies and that citizens keep a sufficient number of fire buckets. It also instructed the militia to take their fire buckets to any fire and report to the fire company officers (while this legislation required the militia to report to the fire company officers, there was still no evidence of any companies at this time). A tax on shopkeepers was authorized to support a night watch. (Dec. 29, 1798, *The Newbern Gazette*)

A regulation imposed in January of 1799 by the aldermen prohibited fires on the wharves after 9 pm at night. The penalty for violating this ordinance was 20 shillings.

By February 1799 there were 14 well pumps in town, each placed under the care of an individual. Pumps were a necessity not only for the routine use of residents and businesses, but also for firefighting. The fire engines required a bucket brigade to fill the "tub" (reservoir of the hand pumper) at working fires. Hand engines developed later on could draft out of the wells. Wells would continue to be drilled well into the 19th century until a water system was established in 1892.

A night watch was re-established to watch for fires and report any suspicious criminal activity. Companies composed of five citizens were established with a captain leading each group. There were penalties for those not reporting for duty on night watch of 20 shillings. Enough watchmen were hired so that no one person would have to perform this duty more than once a month. The watch ran until daylight. Authority was also given to "two officers of the fire companies together with one or more Justices of the Peace… complete power and authority to direct and cause such house or building…" to be blown up with powder…" to prevent the spread of fire. While this authority was granted to the commissioners of New Bern by the North Carolina General Assembly, there was still no evidence of any fire companies having been formed. (Dec. 29, 1798 *The Newbern Gazette*)

**1800s** (Some of the information in this section, unless otherwise noted, is from the meeting notes of the city aldermen)

A contract for the purchase of 100 leather fire buckets was issued on September 12, 1801.

April 1803 saw an order for fire hooks, leather buckets for the fire engines and a repair order for the engines.

William Tignor was reappointed to oversee the fire engines in 1804 for $12/year (he served in this role until 1807). The fire engine house was repaired. Still there was no organized fire company.

Town pumps continued to be built in the early 1800s. Penalties were established for fire code violations. As an example, there was a fee of 5 pounds for baking ovens within 100 feet of wooden buildings.

In November 1805, John Trevercaria, James McKinley, William Johnston, Edward Pasteur, Francis Hawks, and Moses Jarvis were appointed supervisors during fires who had the authority to blow-up houses to halt the spread of fires. Citizens could be fined $5 for disobeying their orders.

Once again, in May 1807 the pumps on the fire engines were repaired at a cost of $185.

February 1808 saw the reduction of the number of night watchmen from 12 to 8. Two shifts were established, one from 9 pm to 1 am, the other 1 am to daylight. This was further reduced to two watchmen to serve from 9 pm to midnight by March of 1809.

There was an authorization for the purchase of a fire engine "of the highest quality" in July 1809 from a company in Philadelphia. Most likely this would have been a double-decker engine which was known as the "Philadelphia style". With this hand pumper, firefighters would stand both on the ground and on the engine to pump (note the platforms on the hand pumper)

Example of Philadelphia-style double-decker hand pumper.    Courtesy *NYC Fire Museum/HV Smith collection.*

In June 1813 the fire buckets and engines were repaired and cleaned. Still no fire company.

On July 1, 1815, David Bascton, Martin Stevenson and John Templeton were appointed captains to establish three fire companies. The city offered incentives for the engine that arrived first at a fire. The captain would receive $10. Fire buckets were repaired and fire hooks made and fitted. Mr. Buxton was paid $50/year to maintain the fire engines. Drag ropes were ordered for the engines so that more men could pull the apparatus.

Commissioners took steps to reduce the risk of fire. In particular, they prevented a blacksmith from erecting a shop in his back yard because of the risk. Other measures were implemented.

In February 1817, the aldermen authorized a penalty of 40 shillings for chimney fires. Fifty fire buckets were ordered for the town and three fire wardens appointed.

Apparently, the three companies established in 1815 were gone by March 1, 1817 as a town meeting was held for the purpose of forming and organizing a fire company. (*Carolina Federal Republican* March 1, 1817)

The three fire engines were placed under the care of T. Gooding for $50/year in 1820.

An act in 1820 by the General Assembly of North Carolina allowed New Bern (and Fayetteville, Wilmington and Tarboro) to accept members of the militia into the ranks of fire engine companies, not to exceed 60. By enrolling in fire companies, the militia-men were exempt from militia duties, except in cases of war, insurrection or invasion. However, Section 3 of this legislation prevented current members of the New Bern Guard, the local militia, from receiving the benefits of this Act. (May 5, 1821 *Newbern Sentinel*)

There was a concerted effort to form several companies as the following newspaper article carried in the *Newbern Sentinel* on June 2, 1821 suggests:

> "Fire Companies-Once More
>
> The members of the fire engine companies are requested to meet at the
>
> Court House, on Wednesday evening next, at 5 o'clock for the purpose
>
> of appointing officers. Books for enlistment are at the Store of Mr.
>
> Forbes, and it is earnestly requested that all persons disposed to unite in
>
> this excellent design will not delay their enrollment."

A fire at 2 am July 9, 1821 in a brick building on Craven Street, functioning as a bakehouse, tested the "new" fire companies. The structure was in the center of a group of wooden homes. It was half an hour before water was being applied by the engines. Fortunately, winds were calm. There was a deficiency of leather buckets, and many of them were useless. The Newbern Guards arrived early and assisted in quelling the fire. (July 14, 1821 *Newbern Sentinel*)

Commissioners once again in 1823 enacted regulations to prevent the building of coopers' shops within 100 feet of another structure. Fines were imposed for chimney fires.

By 1826 demands appeared in the newspapers for an efficient fire company to be formed. An article in the December 9 issue of the *Newbern Sentinel* proclaimed "Our Commissioners are entitled to the thanks of the inhabitants for the disposition they manifest to guard against the destructive ravages of fire; but unless an efficient Fire Company be formed, Fire Engines will, in the hour of extremity, be of comparatively little use."

Fire broke out on Middle Street just south of Pollock Street around 3 am on April 4, 1828 and spread to several homes before being extinguished by a bucket brigade formed by citizens. There was no engine or fire company present. In an article in the April 5th edition of the *Newbern Sentinel*, "the active and efficient" efforts of the black population in extinguishing the fire was acknowledged."

There was a move in 1828 to repeal the General Assembly's Act of 1820 which limited fire departments to a maximum of 60 militia members. As explained earlier, the militia-men were exempt from militia duties, except in cases of war, insurrection or invasion when they enrolled in a fire company. A committee recommended that each fire company be commanded by a Captain and two engineers. For the first time New Bern aldermen proposed a Constitution to govern the fire companies. Article 1 stated each company would be composed of 20 members. Each member had to be at least 15 years old. Article 2 concerned monthly meetings for the purpose of exercising the engine. Article 3 said each company would have a Captain, two Engineers, a Secretary and Treasurer, to serve 1 year. There were procedures for filling vacancies and a chain of command as well as operational procedures (response to fires). (Apr. 26, 1828 *Newbern Sentinel*)

The *Newbern Sentinel* issue of April 26, 1828 published the by-laws as well as a list of the officers for Fire Companies No. 1, No. 2, No. 3 and the Volunteer Company. The same article listed the membership roles for each company except the volunteers. With each company composed of 20 members, the total strength of the department would be 60 militia members plus Company 4 made up of other volunteers.

A new engine was purchased in June,1829 and stored in a newly built engine house near the residence of John Stanly on George Street. The keys to the building were left with 2 members. (June 27, 1829 *Newbern Spectator*)

An early morning fire on July 2, 1835 leveled every building between the Newbern Bank on Craven Street and Mr. Primrose's residence on Pollock Street, a total of 6 stores, 5 store-warehouse combinations, and 3 dwellings and other outbuildings. Damage was estimated at $50,000. (July 3, 1835 *The Weekly Standard*)

On April 17, 1843, at about 2pm, a fire started at the Wade Mill at Union Point. Strong southeast winds blowing at near gale force spread the fire to a warehouse and a building on South Front Street. By mid-afternoon there were fires in 20 different sections of town. Winds eventually changed to a westerly direction (in this case it would be from the west) which helped to stop the progress of the fire. The fire destroyed everything on East Front Street and on Pollock Street up to Craven. Fifty dwellings and buildings, eight stores, thirteen warehouses, a mill and a bakery were destroyed at a loss exceeding $100,000. (Apr. 26, 1843 *The Weekly Standard*, Raleigh.)

Another early morning fire occurred on October 5, 1843 in Mr. T. Williams store on Craven Street which spread to Pollock Street. Brick buildings stopped the spread further, but not before 6 stores and several dwellings lay in ruins. Two of the fire engines damaged in the April fire were still out of service at the time of this fire. (Oct. 11, 1843 *The Weekly Standard*)

Once again the fire department was reorganized in 1845 with the formation of the Atlantic Hook and Ladder Company No. 1 and the Neuse Fire Company No. 2. Both were chartered in 1847. [Note: The Atlantic Company is the *oldest active* chartered fire company in North Carolina as it retains its charter to this day]. The Atlantic had a hand pumper. The Neuse Company received a new hose carriage made in New York in June 1847. A fire on January 13, 1849 destroyed the Turpentine Distillery of Mr. Amos Wade about a mile north of Newbern on the Neuse River. Both the Atlantic and Neuse companies were on the scene but because of the nature of the materials involved, little could be saved. (Jan. 16, 1849 *The Newbernian and North Carolina Advocate*)

The Neuse Fire Co. No. 2 took part in the monthly parade of fire companies in early June 1849 followed by the annual election of officers on June 4th. The 4th of July parade in 1852 featured the Atlantic Fire Company and Neuse Fire Company along with town authorities, the Newbern Amateur Brass Band and Revolutionary Soldiers. (June 29, 1852 *The Newbernian and North Carolina Advocate*)

An accidental fire on January 21, 1852 destroyed Blackwell's new steam sawmill at a loss of $11,000. A brutally cold night froze the fire engines. Firemen confined the fire to the mill. (Feb. 6, 1852 *Raleigh Times*)

A kitchen fire that broke out near the roof of a home on Middle Street around 10 pm September 13, 1852 threatened to spread to nearby structures but the prompt action of the Neuse Fire Company No. 2 and the Atlantic Company No. 1 extinguished the fire and saved the structure. (Sep. 14, 1852 *The Newbernian and North Carolina Advocate*). There was a resolution in the *Newbernian and North Carolina Advocate* on September 24, 1852 thanking the Atlantic and Neuse Fire Companies for "... preserving the town from a destructive conflagration on the night of the 13th..."

The April 23, 1853 edition of *The Weekly News* listed the fire company officers for the Atlantic Co. No. 1, Neuse Co. No. 2, and the newly formed Union Co. No. 3 along with the fire wardens. John D. Flanner was Foreman of the Atlantic, John D. Whitford, Foreman of the Neuse and James E. Morris, Foreman of the Union. The following month the Neuse Fire Company held their annual elections and chose James W. Carmer as their Foreman.

A fire broke out at 2 pm on September 13, 1853 at the turpentine distillery of William Moore on the Trent River near the Long Wharf. There was a delay in the alarm but the Atlantic and Neuse engines arrived promptly checking the progress of the fire. Many of the citizens of the town pitched in to assist the firemen. The Union engine arrived at a later time. (Sep. 17, 1853 *The Weekly News*)

Arson fires became a problem in December 1854 when three blazes of suspect origin struck. The first on December 4th destroyed the Furniture, Saddle and Harness Stores, Carriage House and Stables on Middle Street. The next day, two houses suffered minor damage when their roofs caught fire. (Dec. 7, 1854 *Fayetteville Semi-Weekly Observer*)

A new fire company emerged at the end of February 1857 known as the Relief Company No. 2. Comprised of young men, they appeared in a parade on March 1 dressed in blue shirts trimmed with white and white pantaloons with belts. We do not know much about this company as there is no record of attendance at any fires. (Mar. 3, 1857 *The Weekly Union*)

An editorial in the November 17, 1858 issue of the *Newbern Daily Progress* was critical of the lack of an organized fire department and night watch. A fire on Sunday morning, November 14, nearly destroyed a building before the fire engines arrived 15 minutes after the delayed alarm was turned in. This despite the fact the town owned four fire engines. The paper urged the return of the night watch.

The tin and sheet iron manufacturing facilities of C.A. Hart & Brothers Company caught fire on January 16, 1861. At the corner of Broad and Middle Street, the ensuing fire spread to the City Restaurant and court house. Citizens fought the fire as there was no fire company present. Fireproof buildings halted the spread of the fire. Damage was estimated at $50,000. (Jan. 23, 1861 *The Spirit of the Age*, Raleigh)

Remains of Court House in 1861 fire. The Court House was located in the middle of the intersection of Broad and Middle Street.   *Courtesy New Bern Historical Society*

Another view of the remains of the Court House  *Courtesy New Bern Historical Society*

Chapter **2**

# The Civil War Years

With the Civil War beginning in early 1861, many of the firefighters with the Atlantic Hook & Ladder Co. #1, Neuse Fire Co. #2, and the Union Fire Co. #3 left to fight for the South. It decimated the fire companies, with only a few older members left in town to fight fires. Cries for help in organizing three fire companies, one for each of the hand pumpers, rang out. The January 21, 1861 edition of the *Newbern Weekly Progress* objected to any local regulations preventing blacks from going to fires.

The Mechanics Fire Company formed in April 1861. A subscription fund was started to raise money to buy a new engine for them. A few members were left from the Neuse Company as they were spotted Saturday morning July 27, 1861 on Pollock Street with their high-pressure engine shooting water over the tallest houses. (July 30, 1861 *Newbern Weekly Progress*)

An alarm of fire on August 19, 1861 sent the Mechanics Fire Company to a couple of small tenements on fire, however there was not a suitable well to draft from and their hose was too short to reach the river. (Aug. 20, 1861 *Newbern Weekly Progress*)

During the Battle of New Bern on March 14, 1862, Union General Ambrose Burnside captured North Carolina's second largest city and closed its port through which the Confederates were getting supplies. The capture of New Bern continued Burnside's success along the Carolina coast. As the Confederates fled the city, they set fire to the Washington Hotel and warehouses along the rivers (see the map of fire locations on page 230). With the aid of Union troops, the fires were quelled. Marshal law was declared.

One of the most fascinating aspects of New Bern's firefighting history is the strong connection to the Volunteer Fire Department of New York (would become FDNY) during the Civil War. William Racey was the assistant provost marshal in New Bern charged with organizing the fire regiment of the Union Army. He was the ex-foreman of the Lady Washington Engine Co. No. 40 and assistant foreman of Engine Co. No. 25 in New York City. On July 25, 1862, he formed the New York Engine Co. No. 1 of New Berne and became the Foreman with William

Ross the Assistant Foreman. They adopted the uniforms of the New York Volunteers, sporting red shirts, black pants and fire caps which they got from New York City. The company was made up primarily of New York firemen, many of whom wanted to escape the cold northern winters. There were no soldiers in the company, but other firemen were clerks and teamsters. The hand pumper given to them was in bad shape with many broken parts. The engine was repaired, however, the rig required a new pipe (nozzle for discharging water) which was obtained from New York. (Aug. 2, 1862 *Newbern Weekly Progress*)

**Hand pumper given to the Union in New Bern**  *New Bern Firemen's Museum and NCSFA*

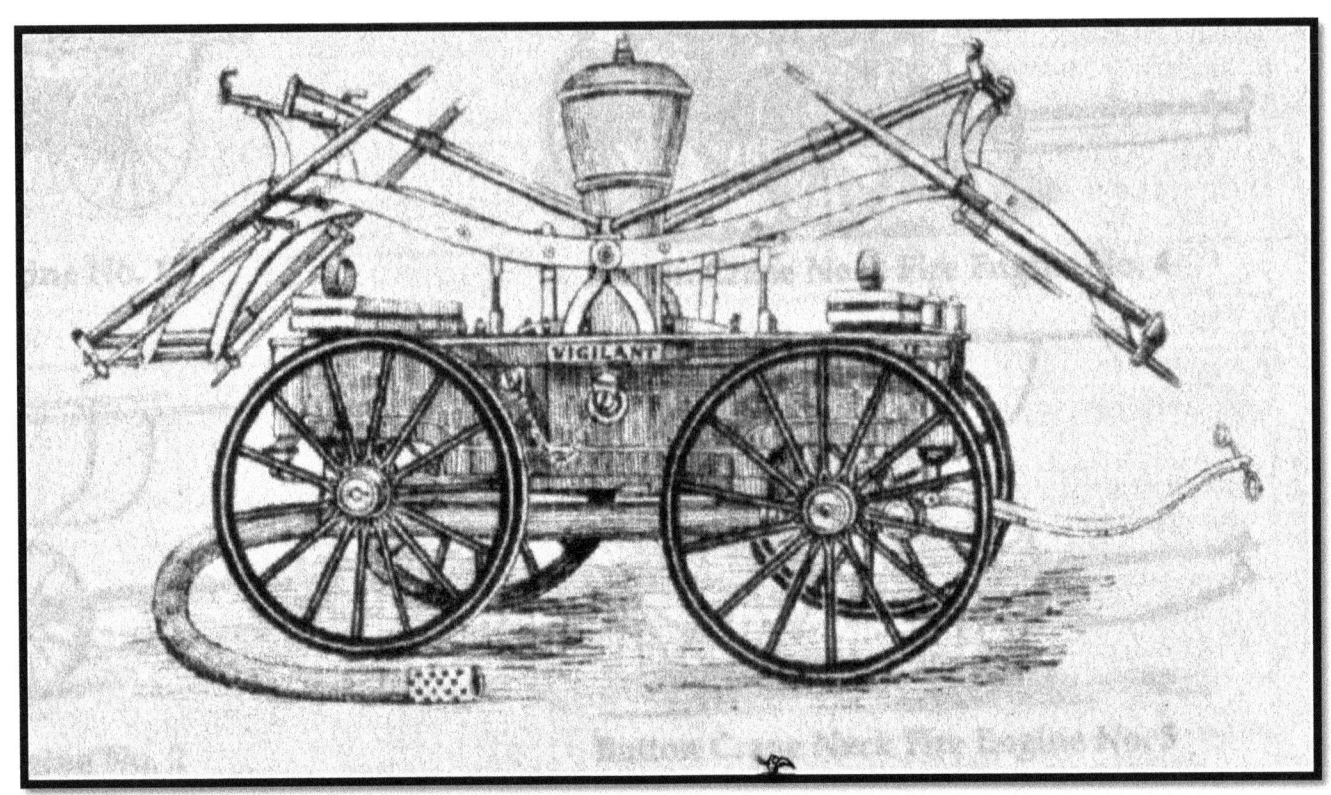

This is the way the engine most likely looked like at delivery.... a double decker manufactured by Merck & Agnew sometime between 1834 and 1860 in Philadelphia.  *Courtesy The Encyclopedia of American Hand Fire Engine*

Also in August 1862, numerous merchants and citizens, who were not enlisted men, formed Hose Company No. 1 which became known as the Foster Hose Co. No. 1. Thirty men were enrolled with Dr. James B. Smith elected Foreman. Their equipment consisted of a hose carriage and buckets. J.G. Foster, Major General of the Volunteers, Jay C. Slaght, Captain and Assistant Quartermaster, and Col. John Kurtz, Provost Marshal were made honorary members of the company. (Aug. 9, 1862 *Newbern Weekly Progress*)

The New York Fire Co. No. 1 of New Bern was renamed the Fire Department of New Berne in 1863 with William Racey elected as Assistant Engineer, J.W. Denny, Chief. Within the New Berne Fire Department were four companies, the John Decker Engine Co. No. 1, named after the New York Chief, the Denny Bucket & Axe Company, the Lady Washington Hook & Ladder Co., named after a fire company in Morrisania (the Bronx), and the Foster Hose Company.

In fire company elections in January 1864, A.B. Norcross was elected Foreman of the Foster Hose Co., P.H. Boyle, Foreman of the Lady Washington Hook & Ladder, and Joseph W. Magrath, Foreman of the "rejuvenated" Atlantic Engine Co. No. 2. The John Decker Engine

Company was disbanded with their engine and equipment turned over to the Foster Hose Company. (Jan. 16, 1864 *The New Berne Times*)

The Second Battle of New Bern was fought from February 1–3, 1864. A garrison of men under the command of Brig. General Palmer repulsed Confederate forces led by Maj. General George Pickett trying to recapture the coastal town which had been lost to the Union Army in 1862. On the first day the entire fire department turned out to relieve the 17th Massachusetts of Provost duty so they could report to the front. On the second day, Assistant Engineer Racey and a crew of firemen captured a rebel crew consisting of an officer and seven men trying to escape by boat. (Feb. 6, 1864 *The New Berne Times*)

In what became an annual parade on Washington's birthday, a parade of fire apparatus and firemen marched through downtown in 1864. For the parade the Denny Bucket & Axe Co. had 30 men in the line of march including the Chief of the department J.W. Denny, the Foster Engine Co. had 61 men, the newly formed Holden Hook & Ladder Co. No. 1 had 63 men, the Atlantic Engine Co. No. 2 with 44 men (it's possible and evidence suggests that the Atlantic Company at this time was composed of Union sympathizers, Northerners and soldiers), and the Lady Washington Hook & Ladder with 40 men. (Feb. 24, 1864 *The New Berne Times*)

On March 6, 1864, John Decker, the Chief of the New York Volunteers visited New Berne. Chief Denny hastily organized a parade with the 2nd Massachusetts band in the lead on Broad Street. Every company in the city turned out. The parade proceeded down Middle, Pollock and Craven streets to the Merchants Bank building. The firefighters of the Denny company were dressed in the red shirted colors of the New York volunteers. Chief Decker gave a short speech. (March 9, 1864 *The New Berne Times*)

April 27, 1864 saw J.W. Denny stepping down as Chief Engineer after being "called to another field of labor" with Lieutenant W.C. Hunt taking over command. On July 22, 1864, George W. Nason, Jr., Assistant Foreman of the Foster Engine Co. No. 1 was elected Chief Engineer of the New Bern Fire Department, replacing Lieut. W.C. Hunt who was deployed back to his regiment. (July 26, 1864 *The New Berne Times*)

A large fire threatened the store-houses of the U.S. government in September 1864. A card of thanks from Wm. I. Palmer, Captain of the Commissary of Subsistence for the U.S. Army, thanked the engine companies and truck company for their work in saving their facilities. (September 29, 1864 *The New Berne Times*). It became customary for anyone receiving service from the fire department to send a "card of thanks", thanking the firemen, to the newspaper for publication.

On November 19-20, 1864 headlines in *The New Berne Times* reported "A Great

Conflagration. Twenty buildings destroyed. Immense loss of property" A fire started in an ice cream Saloon and Fancy Bakery on Middle Street and spread to businesses on Broad Street. The fire on Broad Street was halted by blowing up two buildings. On Middle Street a building was blown up to stop the fire, but to no avail. A second attempt was made by dynamiting another store in the fire's path, which worked. Colonel Poor, the Provost Marshall, was present and "... bagged a large number of light-fingered persons". Brigadier General Palmer and his staff were on scene to provide assistance with firefighting. City crews were short-handed because of the "late sickness" (yellow fever, which was fatal to many firemen). The loss totaled $75,000.

Acting Chief William Ferrett and the foremen of the fire companies formed a committee to meet with Colonel Poor, Chief Provost Marshal for the District of North Carolina, to reorganize the fire department of New Bern in December 1864. (December 8, 1864 *The New Berne Times*)

By January 1865 only the Foster Engine Company (with very few members), Holden Hook & Ladder and Lady Washington Hook & Ladder were left in the city. (Jan. 7, 1865 *The New Berne Times*).

Two black companies, the Harland Fire Company No. 1 and the Kimball Fire Company No. 2 formed in late January 1865. (More information in Chapter 4 "Black Fire Companies")

To ensure safety from fire, Brig. General Palmer and Lieutenant Col. Walter S. Poor established new regulations for stove pipes and chimneys in January 1865. Also, for the recent large fires that occurred which had threatened Union storage facilities, and the lack of adequate fire equipment, Brig. Gen. Palmer ordered a steam engine, hose carriage and additional hose from the Amoskeag Company of Manchester, New Hampshire. (January 31, 1865 *The New Berne Times*)

On March 21, 1865 Lt. Col. Poor reported that the new 550 gallons per minute (GPM) steamer (known as the "Palmer" engine) would be shipped by March 25th. A new fire company made up of Union soldiers, known as the Palmer Steam Engine Co. No. 1 (actually this was the New Bern Steam Fire Engine Company No. 1), was formed to receive the "Palmer" steamer. (March 21, 1865 *The New Berne Times*)

A parade on April 3, 1865 highlighted the toll yellow fever had taken on the firemen. The Holden Hook & Ladder had lost many of their members as did the Foster Hose Company. Only the Palmer Steam Engine Co. and Lady Washington Hook & Ladder showed up dressed in uniforms with a good number of firefighters. The Palmer Co. was pulling a hand pumper as their steamer had not arrived yet. (Apr. 4, 1865 *The New Berne Times*)

The Amoskeag steamer arrived on April 25th. "It was well built, and looks like a perfect beauty" according to the April 28, 1865 *New Berne Times*. An open house took place at the Palmer firehouse on Craven Street next door to the *Times* building.

General Palmer was relieved of command in New Berne in late May and left for Norfolk on June 3, 1865. General Paine replaced him. Palmer returned to the city later to close up his business. (June 3, 1865 *The New Berne Times*)

The *New Berne Times* noted on June 21, 1865 that the two hook & ladder companies had disbanded, or "nearly so". One of the two ladder trucks was sold in October as Chief Engineer Ferrett noted that the city only needed one.

There was an impressive display of the Amoskeag steamer's capabilities on September 9th in which the September 11th 1865 issue of the *New Berne Times* referred to the engine as "a jolly old Squirt".

It was reported that three fire companies were organizing in October 1865. One of these was the New Bern Steam Fire Engine Co. No. 1 which was formerly known as the Palmer Engine Company. With General Palmer gone, the name of the engine company was changed. The charter for the New Bern Steam Engine Company No. 1 shows an organizational date of January 1, 1865 and a charter date of December 20, 1865. (Oct. 4, 1865 *The New Berne Times*)

The provisional (military) government in New Bern was discontinued on February 13, 1866 by order of Colonel W.W. Wheeler.

Two firemen, unknown date.  Fireman on left appears to be wearing a Chief Engineer's cap.  *New Bern Firemen's Museum Collection, photo by Wooten*

# Chapter 3

# Post Civil War to 1900

The aldermen appointed N. Keilton as an inspector and engineer of the New Bern Steam Company in March of 1866 with a salary of $100 per month. The Pell house building was extended to accommodate a hook and ladder in addition to the steamer.

With the war over, many of the soldiers in the New Bern Steam Co. returned home. During the war, many businessmen from New York and elsewhere came to New Bern to help support the troops. They became the nucleus of the postwar Steam Company. The June 30, 1866 edition of *The New Berne Times* reported that the "majority of its members are merchants, and all of them gentlemen of refinement and ability."

The Amoskeag steamer was originally pulled by hand. This required a large number of soldiers to pull the rig as it weighed nearly 6000 pounds. In July 1866, Mr. Dennison offered to keep a pair of horses at his house to pull the steamer if the city would pay for the oats. The city agreed and authorized up to $15 per month for oats.

A fire in the early morning hours of September 16, 1866 destroyed the C.A. Nelson and Company furniture store on Middle Street between Broad and Pollock. The fire spread on both sides of Middle Street and extended to a block of Pollock Street. The demolition of buildings to create a firebreak brought the fire under control with a loss of $200,000. Also destroyed were the J.S. Stevenson & Bro. Dry Goods, John McCormick buildings, Leopold Dry Goods, H. & B. Dry Goods, McNamara & O'Connor Saloon and Restaurant, Henry W. Jones & Co. Dry Goods, John J. Schillinger Lager Beer Saloon, E.H. Lawlor Dry Goods and Groceries, and E. Montanus Cigar and Tobacco. An investigation revealed that the fire was incendiary in nature. A $1500 reward was offered by the city for the arrest and conviction of the party or parties who set the fire. (Sep. 19, 1866 *The Daily Journal*, Wilmington)

Once the southern soldiers came back from the war, the Atlantic Fire Company reformed in 1866 with Captain Joseph Myers as Foreman. Their hand engine was repaired because of several years of neglect. (Sep. 29, 1866 *The New Berne Times*)

From minutes of city aldermen:

September 27, 1866... $1500 appropriated for the purchase of a steam engine. This was because of the ongoing dispute with the U.S. Army over the Amoskeag steamer.

With the ending of the war, controversy erupted over the ownership of the Amoskeag. The steamer belonged to the U.S. government, however General Palmer had instituted a tax on imports and licensing fees on businesses by military order to recoup some of the cost. The citizens of New Bern thought the equipment was for them, but the government claimed it. Captain Stubbs was appointed on behalf of the U.S. government to sell the steamer which he did on October 17, 1866. A group of firefighters stepped forward and re-bought the steamer for $4,750. The October 18, 1866 *The New Berne Times* reported that it had not, "lately seen a happier set of fellows than the company were when they came dragging the machine back to its house—they crowed manfully, the drummers having literally beat the heads out of their drums, and when the old engine was back in its place, they all joined in three cheers..."

There were eight cisterns throughout the city for the Amoskeag steamer to draft from. Locations included the corner of Middle and Pollock, Broad and Middle, New and George, Metcalf and Johnson, Middle and South Front, Bern at Five Points, North Craven (Griffith) at Pelletier's Knitting Mill, and at the Brinson home.

Naturally, there was friction between the southern boys of the Atlantic Company and the northern boys of the New Bern Steam Fire Company. This would continue for many years, into the 20th century, and even in the design of a new fire station in 1928 (more about that later). In addition, the way chiefs were elected in the New Bern Fire Department was a function of this friction (more about this later).

During January 1867, the New Berne Steam Fire Engine Co., Atlantic Engine Co No. 1, and Holden Hook & Ladder Co No. 1 merged to form the Fire Department of the City of New Berne.

From the minutes of the aldermen:

> May 10, 1867.... Engineer of New Bern Steam Company to be paid $75/month.
>
> July 22, 1867... $425 allocated for an engine house for the Atlantic Company
>
> October 14, 1867... $150 for repair of the Atlantic Hook and Ladder.

November 25, 1867.... $150 for repair of the Holden hook & ladder truck.

December 26, 1867... New Bern Steam Fire Engine Co. asked for an appropriation of $175/month. Referred to the fire department committee. In February 1868, commissioners agreed to $135/month. New Bern Steam Fire granted approval for a bell tower.

Fire officers elected in 1869 include Chief Engineer William Brinson, First Assistant William Phillips, Second Assistant Thomas Powers, Foreman of the Holden John Manix, Foreman of the Atlantic John L. Watkins, and Foreman of the New Berne Steam W.G. White.

August 15, 1869.... Chief Engineer Brinson requested that the fire bell be moved to the police station. Granted. The Atlantic Co., adjoining the police station, proposed to extend their station 18'. Granted.

December 13, 1869... Schlacter house on Metcalf St. rented for the newly formed black Reliance Hose Company.

March 7, 1870... $1500 budget for the fire department for the year.

Fire broke out at Hahn's Bakery around 9:30 pm on January 10, 1871. The shingled roof of Christ's Episcopal Church caught fire and spread to the interior and structures on Craven and Pollock Streets. Fighting the fire on both sides of the street proved too much for the steamer. Because of this, fire officials saw the need for another steamer.

**1870 Membership Certificate signed by Chief Engineer Radcliff** *New Bern Firemen's Museum Collection*

**(Left) Remains of Christ Episcopal Church after January 10, 1871 fire.**
New Bern Firemen's Museum Collection

At a monthly meeting of the Atlantic Company on February 6, 1871, the members voted to allow the Reliance Bucket and Axe Company to use their hand engine. (Feb. 8, 1871 *The New Berne Times*)

On April 12, 1871 at around 2 am, a second, more destructive fire struck Hahn's Bakery and the dry goods portion of the city at the corner of Pollock and Middle Street. By 6 am "every building from the residence of Moses Patterson, Esq., on Middle Street, to the National Bank on Pollock Street, was entirely consumed…crossing Middle, the fire seized upon the wooden cornice of the otherwise almost fire proof brick store of Messrs. Weinstein & Bro. This fine building was soon destroyed." The fire destroyed nineteen stores, offices and dwellings. The loss was placed at $225,000. (Apr. 18, 1871 *The Charlotte Democrat*)

After this fire came more calls for enough funds to outfit the fire department with the necessary equipment. The May 7, 1871 edition of *The New Berne Times* asked the city to at least approve the requested funds of the Chief Engineer to purchase a thousand feet of new hose, a jumper (hose cart) for the Reliance Co., buckets and axes for the Excelsiors (the junior firefighters) and have at least 12 more artesian wells drilled. The paper states that "the false cry of 'low taxes' has prevented a tax being laid on the property for this purpose. The unsightly ruins that present themselves to our view, in passing about our city, is a sad commentary on the penurious policy which has kept our fire department in the condition it now is…".

In early June 1871, the New Bern Steam Fire Engine Company moved into their new firehouse on Broad Street. The doors of the engine house were built on the "New York engine house pattern being heavy and grated with a neatly designed cast iron grating." (June 7, 1871 *The New Berne Times*)

**Amoskeag in front of firehouse 300 block of Broad Street**  *Courtesy of the State Archives of North Carolina*

The fire department admitted the Excelsior Fire Co. in 1871. Their company house was the Lane building, adjoining the Holden House on Middle Street. The Excelsiors were junior firefighters 16-18 years old. Upon reaching the age of 18 they could join either the Atlantic or New Bern companies. (June 18, 1871 *The New Berne Times*)

A budget request in July 1871 asked for $900 to pay the salary of an engineer and fireman for the steam engine, $625 for 500 feet of hose, $250 to repair the Holden Hook & Ladder house and $150 for a carriage to carry the Excelsior Company's equipment. The members of the Excelsior Company had raised enough money on their own to purchase buckets, axes and uniforms. (July 12 *The New Bern Times*)

In February 1872, a new hook and ladder carriage for the Excelsior Fire Company No. 4 was completed, built by Mr. Albertson of Middle Street. (Feb. 17, 1872 *The Republic and Courier*)

A fire on October 11, 1872 destroyed the Stimson Steam Saw Mill and nearly all of the machinery, including a large lot of lumber ready for shipment. "The fire department outdid themselves in their efforts to save property, and to the Reliance (Hose Co.) is accorded the praise of the community for their gallant exertions." (Oct. 12, 1872 *The New Berne Times*)

In a report to the city in January 1873 Chief Engineer West gave a description of the fire department and detailed the nine calls during the previous year. This included a store and two homes on January 7, a disastrous fire in the W.H. Manley Bakery on Craven Street January 18th which spread to a harness and shoe shop, drug store and two stores on Pollock Street, an arson fire on May 21 at the millinery shop on Pollock Street, another incendiary fire on July 3rd on Queen Street which destroyed a school and church, the total loss of the Simpson sawmill at the foot of King Street on October 11th and on December 18th the White & Brothers store on Broad Street which spread to a hotel and dwelling. (Jan. 9, 1873 *The New Berne Times*)

The Fire Department Board approved the expenditure of $250 in August 1873 for the purchase of a double-decked engine for the Excelsior Fire Co. No. 4 (Aug. 6, 1873 *The New Berne Times*)

A report to the city in January 1874 by Chief Engineer Radcliff detailed the health of the four companies. The New Bern Steam Engine Company had one steamer in good condition, one hose carriage in good condition, one hose jumper in bad order, 800 feet of hose in good order, 100 feet in bad condition, 400 feet worthless, 1 axe, 8 wrenches, 6 lanterns and 33 certified members. The Atlantic Hook & Ladder Company No. 1 had a truck in good condition with 4 lamps, 3 axes, 24 buckets, 3 ladders, 8 small hooks, 1 large hook with chain, all in good condition. There were 41 certified members. The Mechanics Hook & Ladder Company had 1 truck in good condition, 6 ladders (2 of which were out of order), 16 hooks (4 out of order), 15 buckets, 3 axes, and 3 lamps in good order. Seventeen certified members. The Excelsior Bucket & Axe Company No. 4 had a truck in good condition, with 16 buckets (2 damaged), 6 axes, 2 ladders in good order. Thirty-eight certified members. (Jan. 10, 1874 *The Republic and Courier*)

On February 26, 1874, the annual parade on the 142nd anniversary of George Washington's birth was led by the newly elected Chief Engineer Thomas A. Green, followed by the New Berne Steam Fire Engine Co., Mechanics Hook & Ladder, Excelsior Bucket & Axe, and Atlantic Hook & Ladder. (Feb. 28, 1874 *The Republic and Courier*) These parades, which became an annual tradition until about 1892, were to also acknowledge Washington as one of the greatest firemen who joined the Alexandria Virginia fire department at 17 and served until his death in 1799.

At a meeting of the Board of Engineers and Officers of the New Bern Fire Dept in June 1874, a resolution was adopted to pay any person arriving at the Steam Fire Engine Company on an alarm of fire with a horse which could haul the engine to a fire, $5.00. The second arriving horse's owner would receive $2.50. (June 9, 1874 *The New Berne Times*)

The Silsby Company of Seneca Falls, NY brought a 600 gallons per minute (GPM) steam engine to New Berne for their consideration and offered the city the option of annual installments toward the purchase of the engine. The city accepted after the representative of Silsby demonstrated the capabilities of the engine. (April 26, 1879 *The Newbernian*) Elijah Ellis donated 2 horses to pull the steamer. His name appears on the side of the steamer, beginning a tradition where the Atlantic Company names their rolling stock after a mayor, former chief, or someone of significance to the company.

On January 21, 1880 at 11:30 pm, two prisoners set the Craven County Jail on fire, destroying the structure. The Atlantic Company got the first stream on the building but to no avail. (Jan. 22, 1880 *Kinston Journal*)

Chief Engineer E.M. Pavie ordered a parade of the Newbern Fire Dept on April 28, 1880 including the black fire companies. The department (including black companies) was comprised of two steamers, two hose carriages, one hand engine, one chemical engine, one hook and ladder and bucket truck, and one hose and bucket company. There were approximately 200 active members. (Apr. 24, 1880 *The Newbernian*)

Line of March:
Newbern Silver Cornet Band
Chief and Engineers of Newbern FD
Newbern Steam Fire Engine Co. No. 1
Mechanics Hook & Ladder Co. No. 1
Atlantic Steam Fire Engine Co. No. 1
Engineers of the Reliance Fire Engine Co. No 1 and Rough & Ready Bucket & Axe Co.
Rough and Ready Bucket & Axe Co.
Reliance Fire Engine Co. No. 1                                    (May 1, 1880 *The Newbernian*)

On September 11, 1882 the fire companies met to take action on the city council's proposal to reduce the salaries of the Engineers. The Atlantic Engineer tendered his resignation but was ruled out of order. The New Berne Engineer resigned and they could find no one willing to accept the lower pay and as a result the company went out of service. (Sep. 12, 1882 *The Daily Journal*)

At 6:30 pm on November 15, 1882, a fire broke out on Middle Street in the roof at Rountree's Store, spreading to the Watson & Daniels icehouse, Wahab's store, Roberts Brothers store, Dr. Bate's office, and Major Hughes' office. The Atlantic Company arrived on the scene four minutes after the alarm was turned in, followed closely by the New Bern Steam Company. Reliance came in with their hand pumper. Streams, two from the Atlantic, two from the New Bern, and one from the Reliance Hose Co. prevented the fire from spreading. (Nov. 16, 1882 *New Berne Weekly Journal*)

On January 1, 1883 at 1:30 am, an "incendiary" fire broke out at Tucker's bar room at Five Points and spread to the Hackburn Brothers building and a house on the other side. New Berne Steam Engine was on the scene and discharging a stream in 7 minutes. The Atlantic arrived about 5 minutes later. The fire was rapidly brought under control. (Jan. 4, 1883 *New Berne Weekly Journal*)

February 1883 Parade order of formation:
New Bern Silver Cornet Band
Chief and Assistant Engineers of New Bern FD
Mechanics Hook and Ladder Co. No. 1
Atlantic Steam Fire Engine Co. No. 1
New Bern Steam Fire Engine Co. No. 1
Star Band
Engineers of the Reliance Fire Engine Co. No 1 and Rough & Ready Bucket & Axe Co.
Reliance Fire Engine Co. No. 1
Rough and Ready Bucket & Axe Co.


Active firemen on the 1st day of June 1883 were exempt from the Poll Tax for the year. (July 13, 1883 *The Daily Journal*)

The newspaper offices of the *Daily Journal* were next door to the Atlantic Fire Company. On one particular fire alarm, the staff observed that when the fire bell rang, they saw the horses rush from their stalls and take their position under the drop harnesses (the Atlantic Company was the first company in the state to use the drop harnesses) even without direction from the driver who was absent. (Oct. 9, 1883 *The Daily Journal*)

As mentioned earlier, there was friction between the two companies and as a result a new tradition started in 1884 for the election of the chief of the entire New Bern Fire Department. The companies would alternate chiefs every year. One year the chief would come from the ranks of the New Bern Steam Company with the assistant chief from the Atlantic Company. The next year the chief would come from the Atlantic Company with the assistant from the New Bern Steam Company. This tradition would condition with only a few exceptions into the 1990s!

Silsby steamer rounding the corner of Middle Street onto Broad during a parade in the late 1800s.  *New Bern Firemen's Museum*

A new 500 gallons per minute (GPM) Button Steam engine manufactured by the Button Company of Waterford, NY was ordered by the city in early August 1884 with delivery expected in 90 days at a cost of approximately $4000, less a trade-in allowance of $1100 for the Amoskeag. (Note: Mounted on top of the Amoskeag steamer on the air dome was a lantern which was inscribed "NewBerne 1". The firemen removed the lantern from the steamer when it was traded in and mounted it on the Button). The Button engine was delivered in mid-October and in a test of its capabilities, threw a stream of water over the restored Episcopal Church's 150 foot spire on October 16. So impressed by the performance of the steamer, the members of the New Bern Steam Company began calling themselves the Button Company. On October. 21st, the fire department conducted a test of the two steamers at the Foster wharf. (Oct. 22, 1884 *The Daily Journal*)

**Button Steamer**  *New Bern Firemen's Museum Collection*

On December 23, 1884 the fire department used the two steam engines to pump water out of the hull of the steamer *Defiance*. They pumped about 250,000 gallons in 4 ½ hours. The *Defiance* was again floating. (Dec 24, 1884 *The Daily Journal*)

In December 1884 the fire department purchased a new hose carriage from Silsby for the Atlantic Engine Co. for $750. (City aldermen minutes)

A new operating procedure went into effect in January 1885. "At the first alarm of the fire bell... the New Bern Company will at once repair to the fire. When the second alarm shall be given, which will be known by the fire bell striking twice, at short intervals, the Atlantic Company will move promptly to the scene... the Mechanics Hook and Ladder Co. will move promptly to the fire at the first alarm... William Ellis, Chief" (Jan. 17, 1885 *The Daily Journal*)

February 2, 1885 saw another change in response. Upon an alarm of fire, both steamers will proceed to the scene. The Atlantic engine will begin the work of extinguishing the fire... the New Berne engine will wait for orders before going to work. Signed by William Ellis, Chief. (Feb. 4, 1885 *The Daily Journal*) [Note: the roles were reversed each month as this notice was in effect only for February]

On March 10, 1885, shortly after midnight, there was a fire at a stove and tinware store on Middle Street near the corner of South Front Street which spread to several buildings before encountering brick buildings on South Front and Middle Street. The fire raged for 3 hours. The Button steamer was at the well near the fire on Middle Street while the Silsby steamer went to the Neuse river and drafted. Early on the well at which the Button steamer was at went temporarily dry forcing them to move to another well on Craven Street near the Atlantics' quarters. Destroyed were Smith & Credle Hardware, a medical office, a grocery dealer, gunsmith, harness maker, another hardware dealer, bar room, barber, tailor, the Central Hotel, livery stables, clothiers, druggist, dry goods and house furniture and millinery. The loss was estimated at $100,000. (Mar. 10, 1885 *The Daily Journal*)

Silsby steamer in front of the fire station.  *Ernest C. Richardson III Collection*

**Silsby steamer drafting out of one of the cisterns in the city.** *New Bern Firemen's Museum Collection*

March 10, 1885.... Annual parade of the Fire Department:

New Bern Silver Cornet Band
Chief Engineer William Ellis and Assistant Engineer
Newbern Steam Fire Engine Co.
Mechanics Hook and Ladder Co.
Atlantic Steam Fire Engine Co.
Excelsior Hose Co.
Rough and Ready Hook and Ladder Co.
Reliance Engine Co. (Mar. 8, 1885 *The Daily Journal*)

On March 21, 1885 at 12:55 AM, a fire occurred at the former Atlantic Steam Engine Co building which was being used by the Excelsiors. The old hose cart of the Atlantic being used by the Excelsiors and 500 feet of hose, plus the trucks, hooks and ladders of the Mechanics Hook and Ladder were saved. The fire extended to a tenement house. (Mar. 22, 1885 *The Daily Journal*)

The aldermen notified the foremen of the Mechanics and Rough and Ready fire companies in early October 1886 that if they did not attend calls with their apparatus, the city would no longer pay rent or any other expenses for them. (Oct. 7, 1886 *The Daily Journal*)

February 28, 1887.... Annual Parade of the fire department:

New Berne Steam Fire Engine Band
Chief Joe Willis and Assistant Engineers
Atlantic Steam Fire Engine Co. No. 1
New Berne Steam Fire Engine Co. No. 1
Mechanics Hook and Ladder Co. No. 1
Excelsior Hose Co. No. 1
New Berne Golden Link Band
Reliance Fire Co.
Rough and Ready Fire Co. (Feb. 22, 1887 *The Daily Journal*)

The Ellis Hose Co. was organized on October 29, 1887 with George Womble, Foreman, Loring Gaskill, Asst Foreman. (Oct. 30, 1887 *The Daily Journal*)

February 22, 1888... Annual parade of the New Berne Fire Dept.
    New Berne Steam Fire Co. Band
    Chief and Assistant Engineers

New Berne Steam Fire Engine Co. No. 1
Atlantic Steam Fire Engine Co., No. 1
Excelsior Hose Co. No. 1
Ellis Hose Co.
New Berne Star Band
Rough and Ready Fire Co.
Reliance Fire Co.

Seven hundred dollars was appropriated in May 1890 for a new boiler for the Button and $40 for the repair of one of the pumps of the Silsby which was "injured" while pumping out one of the fire wells. The Chief also recommended that a building be erected to the rear of the city's buildings for the use of the Rough and Ready and Mechanics Hook and Ladder companies. (May 10, 1890 *The Daily Journal*)

On February 13, 1891 at 10:40 pm a terrific explosion rocked the city as the boiler of the Major A. R. Denison Gin and Oil Mill exploded killing two men and scattering debris outward over a square and a half from the mill. Cotton bales caught fire. While Chief Pavie and several other firemen were inside fighting the fire, they narrowly escaped death as the rest of the building came crashing down. The fire department prevented the spread of the fire to other buildings. Damage was $20,000. (Feb. 14, 1891 *The Daily Journal*)

In June 1891, Engineer Warters of New Berne Steam Fire reported on leaks and other defects in the Button's boiler to city aldermen. The city authorized the repairs to be made. Much of the problems with the steamers were from the stress of competitions around the state and some of the methods used to get a "quick" steam. (June 7, 1891 *The Daily Journal*)

On August 11, 1891, Chief E.M. Pavie passed away. The firemen had elected him Foreman of the NBSFE Co 1 in 1870 and he served as Chief in 1880 and again in 1886, 1888, and 1891. Born in New York City in 1837, he was a successful architect and builder in New Bern. (Sep. 16, 1891 *The Daily Journal*)

August 13, 1891... Funeral for Chief Pavie. Order of procession ahead of the hearse:
    City Marshall and policemen
    Prof. Cook's Cornet Band
    New Berne Steam Fire Engine Co.
    Atlantic Steam Fire Engine Co.
    Royal Arcanum
    Royal Order of Good Fellows
    City Council
    Chief Pavie's empty buggy and horse, draped in black

    Hearse
    Deceased's family
    Citizens                                                        (Aug.14, 1891 *The Daily Journal*)

A fire on December 29, 1891 at 1 am in a two-story grocery and general merchandise building on Broad Street spread to other buildings on the corner of Broad and Fleet. This fire showed the need for a water system in the city. The well-used by the first steamer was too close to the fire. In addition, a portion of the well casing had rotted away and had fallen in obstructing access to the water. (Dec. 29, 1891 *The Daily Journal*)

February 24, 1892.... Fair parade line of march with the Governor
    Chief Marshal
    E.K. Bishop and Assistants
    New Berne Steam Fire Engine Co. Band
    New Berne fire engine company steamer decorated with evergreens and streamers
    Excelsior Hose Co. and reel
    Atlantic Steam Fire Engine Co. steamer decorated with evergreens and surmounted by a large hornet's nest
    Atlantic hose carriage with Governor T.M. Holt, William Dunn, President of the Fair Assoc and W.W. Clark, director and manager of the Fair.
    Citizens in buggies and on horseback
    Golden Link Band                                (Feb 25, 1892 *The Daily Journal*)

Fire at the Points on July 21, 1892 destroyed the Richardson & Snelling grocers. It took 15 minutes for parties running down the street to get the alarm turned in at the station. The Atlantic Company had not yet returned from competition in Asheville and the horses of the New Bern Company balked, delaying their response by 30 minutes. The Atlantic hose carriage reached the scene first followed by the New Bern hose carriage. Within a couple of minutes they had hoselines on the fire, but not before it had spread to another grocery store. (July 22, 1892 *The Daily Journal*)

The Mechanics H & L Co was disbanded in mid-1892. In a July 23, 1892 issue of *The Daily Journal*, they urged the formation of a hook and ladder company

The steam engines were used for other purposes as noted in the May 20, 1893 *The Daily Journal*. The Atlantics' Silsby was used to clean out the street pumps. Upon completion of this it was taken to the J.H. Crabtree & Co. shop to have the boiler replaced with a new one which had arrived a few weeks earlier.

An interesting article in the October 23, 1893 edition of the *New Berne Weekly Journal* told of finding powder in the fire engine. The Button steamer was not working up to par, so the firemen gave it a good cleaning out. Four packages of gunpowder were found amounting to about 6 ounces along with ammonia mixed with the water in the boiler. "The positioning of the packages showed that someone familiar with engines had placed them there." They feared that the ammonia could have generated gas that might have resulted in a boiler explosion. The engineer was suspended even though he was not aware of the situation.

By May 1894, the water works system in the city was composed of seven miles of pipes and mains between six and twelve inches in diameter and 75 fire hydrants. (May 6, 1894 *The Daily Journal*). Early streets in New Bern were paved with oyster shells but once the water system was installed, the city paved the streets with bricks.

At an aldermen meeting in June 1894, the Fire Department Committee recommended that the Atlantic hose carriage house be tendered to the New Bern company for their engine and hose carriage. The driver could occupy one of the sleeping apartments. The newly formed Fifth Ward Hose Co. No. 1 petitioned for a hose reel. (June 23, 1894 *The Daily Journal*)

Chief W.D. Barrington announced the following Water Works fire alarm signals in July 1894: 1 tap, keep stand-pipe pressure up; 5 taps, pump direct through main; 2 taps, shut off direct pressure and pump in stand-pipe; 3 taps, fire out. (July 29, 1894 *The Daily Journal*)

A parade of the fire "laddies" on October 14, 1895 featured four "magnificent" percheron horses pulling the two steamers. The horses were furnished by M. Hahn & Company for the occasion to show the capabilities of the horses bred for heavy work. (Oct. 15, 1895 *The Daily Journal*)

In the Grand Parade in August 1897, the two companies displayed brand new hand reels in nickel and brass finishings and ball bearing axles along with the year-old New Bern hose wagon and the brand new Atlantic hose wagon just completed by G.H. Waters and son. The New Bern wagon was pulled by Old Jim and the Atlantic's by a black and bay horse. Mayor William Ellis who held nearly every position in the Atlantic Company led the teams. (Aug. 1, 1897 *The Daily Journal*)

Chief of Department Lee Taylor in 1897.     *New Bern Firemen's Museum Collection.*

**New Bern Steam Engine Company 1896 Hose Wagon built in Raleigh**   *Photo by Andrew Bartholf*

**Atlantic Steam Engine Company 1897 hose wagon built by Waters Buggy & Carriage of New Bern.**
*Photo by Andrew Bartholf*

**Thomas White, driver of one of the hose wagons.**
*New Bern Firemen's Museum Collection*

**Atlantic hose wagon in front of Waters factory. The building was located next to where the present day Museum sits.**
*New Bern Firemen's Museum Collection.*

At 4 AM on January 31, 1898, box alarm 56 was transmitted for a fire at the Union Telegraph office under the Hotel Ohattawka. Damage to the office was extensive. The fire did not spread to the hotel because of the prompt arrival of the fire department. (Feb. 1, 1898 *The Daily Journal*)

## REPORT OF COMMITTEE ON RESOLUTIONS.

*Be it Resolved by the North Carolina State Firemen's Association:*

First. That this Association has heard with profound regret and sorrow that since our last meeting our friend and brother firemen, WILLIAM T. MCCARTHY, of the Atlantic Company, of Newberne, has been called from our midst by the hand of the Almighty.

Second. That in the death of WILLIAM T. MCCARTHY this Association has lost a member whom we have ever found true to our ideal of a fireman and a man; one who has endeared himself to us all by his devotion to duty and simple, manly worth.

Third. That we deeply sympathize with his family, his friends and his company in their great loss and assure them that his memory will ever live in this Association.

Fourth. That a page of our minutes be set aside and these resolutions be spread thereon; that a copy be published in our official organ, *The Volunteer Fireman*, and that a copy be sent to his family with the assurance of our heartfelt sympathy.

R. D. DOUGLAS,
Chairman Committee.

(Left) Resolution from the tenth annual convention of the North Carolina State Firemen's Association in Goldsboro July 26-28, 1898 concerning the death of 27 year-old Atlantic firefighter W. T. McCarthy on March 25, 1898. He was also a Senator representing Craven County in the state legislature. Courtesy NCSFA.

As of August 1899, the New Bern Fire Co. No. 1 owned a fire engine (steamer), hose wagon and a hand reel.

# Chapter 4

## Black Fire Companies

After emancipation and near the end of the Civil War, black leaders felt a need to support the city through voluntary groups. To assist the white volunteer fire companies, two black companies were formed in 1865. John R. Good and Edward A. Richardson formed the Harland Company No. 1 with William Petteford as Chief Engineer. John Randolph Jr. was the foreman and John Bryan, Assistant Foreman of the Kimball Company. They were responsible for the outer areas of the city and to support the "downtown" companies (New Bern Steam, Atlantic and eventually the Holden Hook & Ladder). Total membership numbered 150 men. Other independent white and black fire companies would form, but the Harland and Kimball companies were the first independent companies in the town. (Jan. 31, 1865 *The New Berne Times*)

An article in the constitution of the Kimball Fire Company stated, "Good firemen, like good soldiers, must be good men, morally as well as physically, and such only should be received in this company." (Jan. 31, 1865 *The New Berne Times*)

In 1869 the two companies merged to form the Reliance Bucket & Axe Co. No. 1. They were recognized as a properly organized fire company in New Bern and authorized to purchase 50 fire buckets and 20 axes. The hand pumper formerly used by the New Bern Steam Co. was given to them to use.

Two of the firefighters from the Reliance Company, Limbo Lewis and James York, were recognized for their outstanding work at a wharf fire June 25, 1869 by the *Newbern Journal of Commerce* in their June 27 edition…. "the conduct of these men deserve the highest encomium…never at any time have we ever seen men strive harder and with more cheerfulness…"

In November 1869, the Reliance Company petitioned to be admitted into the New Berne Department. On a vote of the New Bern fire companies (Atlantic, New Bern Steam and Holden), they were turned down based on "color" with the "northern" company (remember, the New Bern Steam Company was comprised mainly of Northerners) voting in the affirmative to let them in. The foreman of the Holden Hook & Ladder, John Manix, resigned rather than vote against the admission as its members had instructed him to do. This subject pitted the *Newbern Journal of Commerce* and *The New Berne Times* against each other with the Journals' editor saying no to admittance, the Times editor arguing for admission. (Nov. 9, 1869 *Newbern Journal of Commerce*)

The Reliance Company reapplied in 1871 and again were turned down. A resolution was drafted and published in the June 18, 1871 issue of *The New Bern Times* which read in part,

> "Whereas, in our rejection, we believe we have been unfairly
> dealt with and not treated as a body of men should be by
> another, who are engaged in the same common cause and
> banded together for the same purpose, and
>
> Whereas, a disposition exists among some of the members
> of one company to disband our organization
> because of such treatment. Therefore, be it
> Resolved That it is our belief that our existence should not
> depend on or be governed in any way by the treatment of man,
> but that being banded together for a high and noble purpose,
> the safety of lives and property, for the extinguishment of
> fires and for general good to the community that we will
> remain in existence so long as the need exists, and while we
> have a sufficient number of members to hold our meetings and
> convey our apparatus to fires.
>
> Resolved, That we ever cheerfully answer to the call of
> duty, and endeavor, by our work and acts, to break down the
> prejudice now existing against us, and which, in our
> opinion, prevents the granting to us of what we conceive to
> be our just rights."

Note: The drivers of the Button and Atlantic hose wagons were black. They were not considered part of the fire department.

On December 13, 1869 the Schlacter house on Metcalf Street was rented for the Reliance Fire

Company. At a meeting of the Atlantic Company in February 1871, they voted to let the Reliance Company use their hand pumper. Reliance received a new hose reel in April 1872. During a trial of the apparatus, they proved that they could reach the top of the highest building in New Bern with a good stream. (May 1, 1872 *The New Berne Times*)

Elections were held in the Reliance Company during December 1872 with John Dixon elected Engineer, Ed. E. Tucker, Foreman, and William L. Rue, Assistant Foreman.

A large parade of black fire companies took place in Raleigh on June 4, 1873 with the Reliance Company attending with their hose carriage. The parade was a temperance demonstration with the purpose to advance the cause among the black population of the state. In attendance from the Reliance Company were E.R. Dudley, W.W. Lawrence, George B. Willis and others. (June 6, 1873 *The New Berne Times*)

On August 6, 1873 the Reliance Bucket & Axe Company traveled to Goldsboro to meet the Brooklyn Steam Fire Engine Company from Wilmington and the Victor and Bucket companies from Raleigh. They wanted to bring the Elm City Band with them but could not afford the $20 expense. (Aug. 1, 1873 *The New Berne Times*)

November 9, 1873 saw the formation of the Rough and Ready Bucket and Axe Fire Company. V.A. Crawford was Engineer, Limber Lewis, Foreman; Samuel Jackson, Assistant Foreman. (Nov. 13, 1873 *The New Berne Times*)

At 5 am on October 16, 1874, fire struck the home of Mr. Hutchinson on Metcalf near Broad Street. The prompt arrival of the Reliance Company prevented the spread of the fire. (Oct. 17, 1874 *The Newbernian*)

The Reliance Company provided assistance to the city on November 15, 1882 when a fire broke out at Rountree's Store on Middle Street and spread to the Watson & Daniels Icehouse, Wahab's store, Roberts Brothers store and several other offices. (November 16, 1882 *New Berne Weekly Journal*)

There was a motion in March 1883 to buy a hand engine for the Reliance Engine Company. They referred the motion back to the Fire Department committee for a report on cost and then to report back at the next meeting. At the June meeting, the city passed on a decision. (June 28, 1883 *The Daily Journal*). An editorial in the paper admonished the city for passing on the decision noting that the Reliance Fire Company "has done good work, that they are equipped firemen, and will do their duty to the city...We believe that justice to the company would be nothing less than an engine"

Periodically black fire companies from other cities would visit New Bern and on July 30, 1884 black companies from Washington and Greenville came to town and used the store at the corner of Pollock and Craven as headquarters. Often competitive events were held between companies. (July 30, 1884 *The Daily Journal*)

The city sold the old hand engine of the Reliance Company at auction on July 2, 1885. (July 19, 1885 *The Daily Journal*)

Apparently the Rough and Ready company was not attending calls in 1886 and if this continued the city notified them they would no longer pay the rent on their quarters or any other expenses. (Dec. 5, 1889, *The Daily Journal*)

In June 1887 the Board of Councilmen recommended a new steam engine be purchased for the Reliance Company since their old hand engine was condemned and sold. The measure was approved, however, the city never purchased a steamer for them. The company disbanded in 1890. (June 9, 1887 *The Daily Journal*)

Limbo L. Lewis, a charter member of the Reliance Engine Company, passed away on July 29th, 1889. A joint resolution of the Rough & Ready and Reliance Engine Company in part stated "Whereas, It has pleased Almighty God in His all-wise providence to remove from our ranks our much beloved fireman…that whilst we bend in humble submission to the expression of Divine Will we sincerely deplore his loss as one not easily replaced, though we at the same time rejoice that our loss has proved his eternal gain." W.W. Lawrence, Elias Hays, Wm. Jones, John Whitfield, Major Bryan, and Nathan Slade signed the resolution. (Aug. 2, 1889 *The Daily Journal*)

Once again the Rough and Ready Company was not attending fires in 1889, but this time it was due to the lack of a horse to pull the hook and ladder. The city made arrangements for a pair of mules to pull the vehicle. (Dec. 5, 1889 *The Daily Journal*)

Another, much less known, black fire company formed in 1894 known as the Fourth Ward Hose Reel (not to be confused with the white Fourth Ward that formed in 1910). One reference to them was in a "Colored Fair Programme" on August 27, 1895 in which they were in the line of march with Foreman Alonso Williams along with the Rough and Ready Company as well as twelve baseball teams and two bands. Another reference was a return from Kinston on May 6, 1897 after helping a black Kinston company celebrate their anniversary. (Aug. 27, 1895 and May 7, 1897 *The Daily Journal*)

In 1895, a brick building opposite J.J. Disosway & Co. underwent changes to adapt the structure for the Rough and Ready Hook & Ladder Co. and their new hook and ladder truck (this was actually the surplus hook and ladder from the city). It would also house a hose cart, horse and a pair of mules to haul the hook and ladder. There would be sleeping quarters for the drivers. (Oct. 3, 1895 *The Daily Journal*)

The Sixth Ward Reel Company formed in early 1898. The city agreed to provide feed for their horse but held off in a meeting in January on providing them with a wagon. In the annual elections of the Sixth Ward Hose Company in June 1900, they elected R.R. Green foreman, J.D. Davenport, assistant foreman, and H.B. Ward, captain of the hose. (Jan. 8, 1898, June 27, 1900 *The Daily Journal*)

Robert Green, captain of the Sixth Ward Hose Reel received twenty-five dollars from the Blades Lumber Company in appreciation of their "able service" at the May 17, 1905 fire. (June 2, 1905 *New Berne Weekly Journal*)

On March 1, 1906 the Cedar Grove Black Church was destroyed by fire. The Sixth Ward Hose Reel Co. prevented the fire from spreading to homes on either side. They received help from the Atlantic and Button Companies. (Mar. 2, 1906 *New Berne Weekly Journal*)

The Sixth Ward Hose Company held their annual elections January 2, 1907 and chose A.P. Davis as foreman, W.B. Aldridge, assistant foreman, and Dorsey Davis, captain of the hose. (Jan. 4, 1907 *The Daily Journal*)

In January 1907 the fire department asked the board of aldermen for a horse for the 6th Ward Reel Co to pull their hose wagon instead of being hand drawn. The 6th Ward answered alarms in the box 58, 54, 55 and 35 area only unless there was a general alarm. By the same token, the "downtown" companies would not answer alarms in these box locations unless they requested their assistance. (Jan. 18, 1907 *New Berne Weekly Journal*)

A severe storm the night of April 1, 1907 blew down the building of the Sixth Ward Hose Reel Company. (Apr. 2, 1907 *The Daily Journal*)

January 1908....A.P. Chapman elected Foreman of the Sixth Ward Fire Company. (Jan. 14, 1908 *New Berne Weekly Journal*). Members of the Sixth Ward Hose Company in 1908: A. P. Dayis, Foreman, W. B. Aldrick, Asst. Foreman; W. A. Williams, Financial Secretary; J W. Martin, Captain of the Hose; Joseph Bryant, Chaplain; John Slade Grant Boyd, Matthew Banks, Henry Lee. W H Pool, J T. Green, Robert Fisher, C.W. Pool, J. E. Henderson, R.T. Gardner, James Bryant, A.P. Chapman, W H. Williams, Lewis Hill, Alonzo Williams, Major Davis

In a sign of the times, separate conventions and competitions were held for the white and black fire companies. At the 1908 convention in Washington, NC, A.P. Davis and J.E. Hudson represented the Sixth Ward Hose Company. New Bern hosted the 20$^{th}$ North Carolina Association of Colored Firemen in August 1909. No less than 26 companies attended. Housing became an issue as public housing in the city was for whites only. The city board donated $50 for entertainment. (Aug. 4, 1911 *New Berne Weekly Journal*)

The Riverside Hose Company organized in June 1911 made up of white citizens of the Sixth Ward. Two months later they asked that the city give the quarters and horse of the Sixth Ward Hose Company to them. In return they would provide their service gratis. At the same meeting the Sixth Ward Company asked permission to use their horse and wagon at the colored foremen's tournament in Elizabeth City. Their request was granted along with $50 for expenses. Fortunately, the city did not side with the Riverside Hose Company. (Aug. 4, 1911 *New Berne Weekly Journal*)

The Sixth Ward Hose Company won first prize in the long-distance reel race in Elizabeth City with a time of 26 seconds. They also won first prize in the grab reel race with a time of 23 seconds and first prize in the hose wagon race with a time of 27.5 seconds. (Aug. 18, 1911 *New Berne Weekly Journal*)

By 1912, with the imminent arrival of motorized equipment in the New Bern department, the Sixth Ward Hose Company closed.

And so ends the history of black fire companies in the city, however, it was not the end of segregation in the city which continued into the 1960s. Unfortunately, there are no pictures of the black companies. This may be due in part to the fire of 1922 which destroyed a large part of the black section of town.

## Chapter 5

# Other Independent Companies

Besides the black fire companies, there were four other white independent fire companies in the period from the 1870s to the motorized equipment in the 1914-1915 time frame. There was also a junior fire company made up of 16-18-year-olds. Members of the junior fire company would join either the Atlantic or Button companies when they turned 18.

The oldest of the companies is the Excelsior Bucket & Axe Co. #4, which was the junior firefighters. They formed in 1871 and were in existence until 1895. Other companies included the Ellis Hose Company which lasted only two years (1887-1888), the Fifth Ward Hose Company (1894-1911), the Fourth Ward Hose Company (1910-1917) and the Riverside Hose Company (1911-1917).

The independent companies covered the outskirts of the city with the Atlantic and Button companies protecting the "downtown" area along with the Holden Hook & Ladder Company (name changed to Mechanics Hook & Ladder in 1873).

In 1871 the Excelsiors formally became part of the New Bern Fire Department and occupied the Lane building adjoining the Holden Hook & Ladder on Middle Street. They received $150 from the city to purchase a carriage to carry their equipment. In addition, the members raised enough money by sponsoring dances and bake sales to purchase their own buckets, axes and uniforms. In August 1873 the city purchased a double-decker hand pumper for the Excelsiors at a cost of $250. (June 18, 1871 *The New Berne Times*)

On March 21, 1885 at 12:55 am, a fire broke out at the former Atlantic Steam Engine Company which was being used by the Excelsiors. Fire crews were able to save the old hose cart of the Atlantic Company used by the Excelsiors and the hook and ladder of the Mechanics. (Mar. 22, 1885 *The Daily Journal*)

The newly organized Fifth Ward Fire Company No. 1 petitioned the city for a hose reel in June 1894. On February 27, 1902, a small fire on Cedar Street was extinguished by the Fifth Ward hose reel before the downtown companies arrived. The horses for the Atlantic and Button companies were six blocks from their quarters at the time of the alarm. New procedures in 1909 called for the Fifth Ward hose wagon on a third alarm in the city. (June 23, 1894 *The Daily Journal* and Feb. 28, 1902 *The Daily Journal*)

The Fourth Ward Fire Co. organized in July 1910 rigging a wagon to haul hose. A month later they requested from the city a horse and a new hose wagon which was granted. Their new hose wagon was constructed by carriage and wagon builder D.H. Williams and delivered on June 21, 1911. (July 28, 1910 *The Daily Journal*)

The last of the companies to organize was the Riverside Hose Company in June 1911, composed of the white citizens of the Sixth Ward. R.H. Dowdy was elected foreman, Helen Huff, Assistant Foreman. In August, Riverside petitioned the city to take the quarters and horse of the Sixth Ward, a black company. In return they stated they would provide their services gratis. The city never acted on this. Riverside received their new hose wagon built by the Waters Buggy Company of New Bern in July 1912. (June 27, 1911 *The Daily Journal*)

Both the Riverside and Fourth Ward fire companies took part in many of the same tournaments as the Button and Atlantic companies from 1912 on. In hose wagon competition in Fayetteville in 1912, the Fourth Ward split second, third and fourth prizes with two Raleigh teams. Riverside took fifth. In Wilmington in August 1913, Riverside won the hose wagon race with the Button Co. second, Atlantic Co. third and the Fourth Ward fifth. During intercity competition in September 1914, Riverside came in first in the hose wagon race followed by the Atlantic and Fourth Ward. The Button Company was disqualified when their hose blew off the hydrant.

In May 1915, a disagreement with the city led to the resignation of all Button firemen effective June 1. Both the Riverside and Fourth Ward companies petitioned the city to take over the quarters and equipment of the Button Company including their 1914 American LaFrance motorized pumper. Fortunately, the dispute was settled with the city and the Button members returned. (May 14, 1915 *New Bern Weekly Journal*)

With the delivery of the second American LaFrance in 1915, there was no longer a need for hand pulled hose reels as the motorized vehicles could cover a greater area and carry a larger amount of hose. This led to the downfall of the independent fire companies. The Riverside Company was the last surviving company when they turned in their horse and closed their doors in 1917.

**Fourth Ward Hose Company**  *New Bern Firemen's Museum Collection*

Chapter **6**

# Notable Fire Chiefs of the 1800s

*William Racey*

William H. Racey.

William Racey joined the quartermaster department as an assistant provost marshal in New Bern after they mustered his company out during the Civil War. They charged him with organizing a fire department in the city. Having experience as a New York City fireman with the Lady Washington Engine Co. 40, he formed companies based on the New York City department. The first company he organized was the New York Fire Engine Co. #1 of New Bern which was staffed by older members of the New York department who had moved south to escape the harsh winters. He later broke this up into four companies in 1862. He created the John Decker Engine Co. #1 named after the fire chief of New York City. The second company was the Denny Bucket & Axe Company named after its foreman John Denny, who also was a New York City fireman. They named the Lady Washington Hook & Ladder after his former company in New York. Rounding out the department was the Foster Hose Company named after Major General J.G. Foster who led the Goldsboro expedition. The firemen named Racey the Chief Engineer of the fire department. Because of illness he returned to New York City in 1864.

## Chief Engineer Edward Pavie

*New Bern Firemen's Museum Collection*

Chief Pavie was born in New York City and moved to New Bern during the Civil War. He was an accomplished and well-respected architect and builder. In his businesses he hired many black artisans and worked with all segments of the population. Pavie formed a partnership with a New Bern builder, Frederick Lane, to become one of the best known contractors in the city. During the 1870s and 1880s there was a building boom in New Bern. In the late 1880s he developed rental properties in the black section of the city which became known as Pavie Town. Among his many projects includes the J.E. Nash store, the Sebastian Bangert Market House in the 300 block of Middle Street, the Baer and Eppler building on Pollock Street, the F. Ulrich House and Saloon on Middle Street, the George W. Claypool House on the corner of Broad and Craven, Hackburn and Willett Store on Pollock, the T.H. Huddleston Office Building on Pollock near Middle and the William Dunn House on Middle just north of Broad. All of his buildings are no longer standing or altered. Unfortunately, a lot of his projects were not documented. His only known surviving work is the stained glass windows he glazed at the Christ Episcopal Church on Pollock Street. Pavie also worked on projects in many other locations in North Carolina.

He served in the capacity of Chief Engineer of the New Bern Fire Department in 1880, 1886, 1888, and 1891 until his untimely death on August 11th of 1891 at 54. A funeral procession through the city was held on August 13 with his empty chief's buggy draped in black. The city council ordered the city bell to be tolled throughout the funeral service. All businesses in the city closed for the day so that everyone could attend.

In a segregated fire department, the Chief held a particular sympathy for the black fire companies, inviting them to take part in the annual Washington's birthday firemen's parade.

Source: *North Carolina Architects & Builders, A Biographical Dictionary* by Lynda Vestal Herzog and Catherine W. Bishir, published in 2000.

Pavie memorial in Cedar Grove Cemetery.  *Photo by Andrew Bartholf*

## *Chief Engineer Samuel Radcliff*

Samuel Radcliff was the longest serving Chief Engineer of the New Bern Fire Department during the 19th century filling the position in 1867-68, 1870, 1873, 1875, and 1878. He was recognized across the state serving as Chair of the Convention of Fire and Military Departments in February 1875. In addition, the Chief was a New Bern Commissioner from 1867 until 1868. In the private sector he owned a steam saw mill at the foot of Pollock Street on the Neuse River. One unfortunate event connected with his mill was the destruction of a new mill being erected on December 6, 1879 when a powerful Nor'Easter struck the New Bern area with strong winds and the highest tide ever recorded at that point in time. His loss was $500 in 1879 dollars.

Mr. Radcliff was also the North Carolina representative of the United States Gas Light Company of New York, the developers of a new patented lamp that burned petroleum spirits which was much less expensive and safer than previous lighting.

**(Left) New Bern Steam Fire Engine Co. firehouse on Broad St. draped in mourning for departed member Clarence A. Radcliff in August 1885, the son of Chief Engineer Samuel Radcliff who died in 1880. "The Son Has Joined The Father"**

The chief died on December 19, 1880 at 57. Two years later in the annual Washington's Day parade, the members of the fire department passed the late residence of Mr. Radcliff with lifted hats out of respect for him. (Feb. 23, 1883 *The Daily Journal*)

Samuel's two sons, Clarence A., and Sam C., were also members of the Button Company. Clarence died in August of 1885 at the age of 25.

Sources: Feb. 17, 1872 *The Republic and Courier*, Feb. 14, 1875 *The Newbernian*. Dec. 10, 1879 *The Daily Review* (Wilmington), Aug. 14, 1885 *Daily Journal*.

Samuel Radcliff Memorial in Cedar Grove Cemetery. *Photo by Andrew Bartholf*

Chapter 7

# Early 1900s

During this period and in the late 1800s, the Atlantic and Button companies were very much family oriented, bringing the circus to town and sponsoring dances to raise money. They formed junior fire companies within the two companies with members as young as 8-10 years old. During the parades, they often transported family members on the apparatus. In return for their service the city would provide funding for the firemen to take outings (vacations).

**Atlantic Company at a parade in the early 1900s, possibly in Wilmington.** *New Bern Firemen's Museum Collection*

Ghent Fairgrounds and casino where the fire companies sponsored dances and the circus. *Courtesy New Bern Historical Society*

A disagreement developed between Chief W. F. Richardson and the Mayor and Chairman of the Fire Committee. The mayor refused to allow the hook and ladder to respond to calls. When the Chief appealed to the public in *The Daily Journal* on July 29, 1900, the mayor's order was eventually overturned.

Box 48 was struck on February 27, 1902 for a small blaze in a house on Cedar Street. The Fifth Ward hose reel had the fire extinguished before the downtown companies arrived as their horses were six blocks from quarters when the alarm sounded. (Feb. 28 1902 *The Daily Journal*)

On July 24, 1902 a large industrial fire erupted at The E.H. & J.A. Meadows Co. Depository for fish and guano on the Neuse River near East Front Street. Firemen confined the fire to the three buildings and prevented the fire from spreading to the rest of the city. (July 25, 1902 *New Berne Weekly Journal*)

Fire destroyed the Trent Lumber Company plant mills and dry kilns and a large amount of lumber shortly before 8 pm on October 31, 1902. Firemen prevented the fire from spreading to the A. & H.O. Railroad Company warehouse by stationing hoselines on the roof and along the dock. Damage was estimated at $20,000. (Nov. 1, 1902 *The Daily Journal*)

A fire during the night of January 13, 1903 destroyed a building owned by Dr. F. W. Hughes which contained the Bradham's Pharmacy, an insurance company, Simmons & Hollowell Company dry goods store and a dental office. The loss was estimated at $20,000. (Jan. 14, 1903 *News and Observer*)

Shortly after 10 pm on July 8, 1903, a fire destroyed more than half a block and several stables, including those of Scott's and Mitchell's. The Planter's tobacco warehouse was reduced to rubble. Damage was estimated at $50,000. Between the 2 steam engines and 2 hose wagons, 15 hose streams were played on the fire. (July 10, 1903 *New Berne Weekly Journal*).

On November 6, 1904, Assistant Chief Johnnie J. Gaskill died at 29 because of complications from a "brief but very distressing illness". He had been sick for two weeks. His exact cause of death is unclear. (Nov. 8, 1904 *The Daily Journal*)

By December 31, 1904 there were 81 fire hydrants in the city. (Feb. 17, 1905 *The Daily Journal*)

Fire destroyed two stores on Pollock Street on March 12, 1905. With the rapid growth of the city, the *New Berne Weekly Journal* recommended a paid fire department be implemented in New Bern. (March 17, 1905 *New Berne Weekly Journal*)

A fire on May 17, 1905 at 12:25 pm gutted the dry kiln of the New Blades Mill along with 500,000 feet of lumber. Brick walls helped to prevent the spread of the fire. The 2 steam engines and hose wagons were providing 15 streams. The Sixth Ward Hose Reel assisted at the scene. Damage was estimated at $50,000. (May 17, 1905 *The Daily Journal*)

The three-story building of Dr. N.H. Street was destroyed in a fire early in the morning of August 28, 1906. The Odd Fellows and the Knights of Pythias also occupied the building. Loss was estimated at $20,000 in what was described as an incendiary fire. (Aug. 29, 1906 *News and Observer*)

The city aldermen in February 1907 ordered a voucher for $60 for Chief J.B. Dawson for his services in 1906. Chief Dawson reported 32 fires in 1906 with a total loss of $44,000. (Feb. 14, 1907 *The Daily Journal*)

On April 2, 1907 at approximately 3 am, a fire broke out at the J.M. Arnold stable on Middle Street. Strong winds carried embers to homes on Pollock Street and west to Hancock Street. The First Baptist Church on Middle Street caught on fire three times, flames being extinguished by a bucket brigade. The Atlantic and Button companies kept the flames from spreading to adjacent sections. Damage was in the thousands of dollars. Ten horses perished. (April 4, 1907 *The North Carolinian*)

**Fire of April 2, 1907**  *New Bern Firemen's Museum Collection*

A large commercial fire in Morehead City destroyed 15 stores on January 30, 1908. New Bern was asked to provide assistance. As the city prepared to load a steamer and the Sixth Ward hose reel on a train bound for Morehead, they were canceled before the train left the station. (Jan. 31, 1908 *The Daily Journal*)

New department rules on February 3, 1909 stated that no person will be allowed to ride on the hook and ladder unless they are a member and only six on the truck. A General alarm will be seven taps of the bells calling for high pressure and the entire department, a third alarm calls for the Fifth Ward hose wagon to the downtown district (it answers no alarm east of George Street and south of Queen Street). The All-Out notification is three taps. (Feb 4, 1909 *The New Bern Sun*)

A fire on November 6, 1909 was discovered at 2:30 am when sparks from the boiler ignited the underside of the roof of the Norfolk Southern Railroad repair shop, destroying the entire structure. Only the paint shop was saved. The loss included the roundhouse, machine shops, blacksmith shops, foundry and planing mill. All the shops were connected which led to the rapid spread of the fire. Also lost were two locomotives, two coaches, two box cars, and two dining cars which had just been finished. The loss was estimated at $200,000. New Bern responded with the Silsby steamer, one hook and ladder, three hose wagons and a supply wagon. Six hydrants within the vicinity of the shops were used. (*Fire and Water Engineering*, Dec. 1909, pp 492-493)

**Norfolk Southern repair shop fire November 6, 1909.**                                                                    Courtesy *Fire Engineering*

**Remains of locomotive** **Courtesy** *Fire Engineering*

Courtesy *Fire Engineering*

**Courtesy *Fire Engineering***

On April 14, 1910, five homes were destroyed by fire early in the morning. The gong at the fire house did not ring, forcing Chief Richardson to go down to the station to wake the drivers and ring the alarm by hand. In addition, the hose in both hose wagons was not long enough to reach the fire from the hydrant. They called the Sixth Ward Hose Company for more hose. By the time they had stretched the lines, the homes were gone. (Apr. 15, 1910 *New Berne Weekly Journal*)

**Button Wagon. Note 27 on side of seat is their record time of 27 seconds in the hose wagon race which dates this to between 1908 and 1911.**
*New Bern Firemen's Museum Collection*

**Another picture of Button wagon in front of the fire station sometime between 1908 and 1911.**
*New Bern Firemen's Museum Collection*

The Fourth Ward Hose Fire Co. was organized in July 1910. They rigged up a hose wagon in their colors of red and white. (July 28, 1910 *The Daily Journal*). The following month they petitioned the city for a horse and hose wagon to replace their rig, which was granted. (Aug. 3, 1910 *The Daily Journal*)

New Bern celebrated its bicentennial July 25-30 in 1910 with a huge floral and industrial parade on Monday, featuring carnival pageants and floats from various North Carolina cities and the state military and naval forces. The parade also featured depictions of great events in the state's history. After a parade on Wednesday, North Carolina firefighters held their tournament in the city with several contests concluding on Friday. (July 29, 1910 *The Daily Times*, Wilson)

**Atlantic Company at the 1910 bicentennial parade**  *New Bern Firemen's Museum Collection*

Button Company at 1910 Bicentennial parade. *New Bern Firemen's Museum Collection*

**1910 Bicentennial Parade in New Bern.** *New Bern Firemen's Museum Collection*

**Atlantic Hose Wagon in 1910 parade in front of Dr. Rhem's house**  *New Bern Firemen's Museum Collection*

On October 31, 1910 shortly after 6 pm, a fire destroyed the Norfolk Southern Railroad Company's Trent River Warehouse with the loss of all freight. Damage was estimated at $75,000. The fire had too much of a head-start for anything to be saved. All companies were on the scene. (Nov. 1, 1910 *New Berne Weekly Journal*)

Around 9 pm on the evening of June 5, 1911, box 61 was struck which turned out to be a false alarm. Shortly thereafter Box 28 was turned in, however no such box exists. Firemen were able to locate the fire in a group of the few remaining wooden buildings in the downtown section on Middle and South Front Street. The Price Market and Coney Island Confectionary stores were destroyed along with a barber shop and a small restaurant. (June 6, 1911 *New Berne Weekly Journal*)

**Atlantic and Button steamers, hose wagon and hook & ladder in 1911 parade.** *New Bern Firemen's Museum Collection*

At a meeting of the aldermen in June 1911, Chief George Harrington requested that a driver be employed to stay at the engine house at all times to be ready to respond with the engines. The Sixth Ward Hose Company requested to hire their own driver. (June 14, 1911 *The New Bern Sun*)

The Fourth Ward Hose Company received a new hose wagon built by carriage and wagon builder, D.H. Williams, in June 1911. (June 22, 1911 *The Daily Journal*)

The Riverside Hose Company was organized in June 1911. This was an organization of the white citizens of the Sixth Ward. R.H. Dowdy was elected foreman, Helen Huff, Asst Foreman. (June 27, 1911 *The Daily Journal*)

**Riverside Hose Company on the corner of National Ave. and Avenue A**  *New Bern Firemen's Museum Collection*

At the August 1911 city meeting, the Riverside Hose Company asked that the quarters and horse of the Sixth Ward Hose Company be given to them. In return they would provide their service gratis. The city did not act on this proposal.

February 4, 1912, shortly before 7 am, fire gutted the Stewart Building on Middle Street with a loss of $40,000. The alarm was turned in at the fire alarm box on the corner of South Front and Middle Street. Police officer Fred Rowe rescued two persons from the second floor including the editor of the Journal after breaking down the door. (Feb. 6, 1912 *The Daily Journal*)

The Riverside Hose Company received their new hose wagon built by the Waters Buggy Works in July 1912. (July 23, 1912 *The Daily Journal*)

The firemen held a Labor Day tournament in 1912. They invited Kinston, Goldsboro and Morehead City. (Aug. 21, 1912 *The Daily Journal*)

During the week of November. 17, 1913, the Atlantic Fire Company sponsored the Smith's Greatest Shows carnival, one of the largest in the country, at the Ghent Fairgrounds. The show included trained animals. (Nov. 9, 1913 *The Daily Journal*)

**Button hose wagon. Note 26 2/5 on side of the seat which was their new best time which dates this picture between 1911 and 1914.**
*Ernest C. Richardson III Collection*

The Riverside Hose Company petitioned the city for an alarm indicator (for fire locations) in early 1914. The request was referred to the Fire Department Committee for action and eventually granted. (Jan. 7, 1914 *The Daily Journal*)

During a city meeting in January 1914, retiring Chief of Department, Thomas Davis, reports that the total fire loss during 1913 was only $12,000, the lowest in the department's history. They elected Thomas Lassiter Chief, and L.R. Tucker, Assistant Chief. (Jan. 10, 1914 *The Daily Journal*)

It was reported on February 13, 1914 that each of the four fire companies was equipped with chemical apparatus to extinguish fires. (Feb. 13, 1914 *The Daily Journal*)

Another fire shortly after midnight on May 4, 1914 destroyed the Ready Wear Garment Company on Pollock Street. With good water pressure, they confined the fire to the building. There was a loss of $10,000 in stock. The horse that pulled the New Bern Steam Company hose wagon had been injured, so Mayor Albert Bangert and three other individuals pulled the wagon from the headquarters on Craven Street around the corner to the fire. (May 4, 1914 *The New Bern Sun*)

Two and a half weeks later, on May 23, a fire completely destroyed the West Lumber and Box Company's Plant on National Avenue with the loss estimated at $125,000. The American Canning Company storage warehouse was also destroyed. A passing locomotive may have sparked the fire. All four companies were on scene and the plants emergency pumps were operating, but to no avail. Seventy cars of lumber were also destroyed. (May 24, 1914 *The Daily Journal*)

The Riverside Co received a donation of $75 from the city for uniforms in June 1914. The New Bern Steam Fire Engine Co. No. 1 offered to donate $1000 toward the purchase of a new motorized engine if the city would assign the new engine to them. The new engine was ordered at a cost of $9000. (June 3, 1914 *The New Bern Sun*).

The rebuilt Fire Alarm System was nearing completion in August 1914. A switchboard and storage batteries were put in place. All new wiring was strung to the fire alarm boxes. (Aug. 7, 1914 *The Daily Journal*)

The new American LaFrance engine arrives in New Bern and is put to the test on November 27, 1914. For two hours the engine was at the corner of Middle and Pollock Streets as streams of water were thrown over the tower of the Federal building. At a pump test at the foot of Craven Street, it flowed 1010 gallons through three lines. After they completed the pump tests, the firemen took the truck on the highway to see how fast it would go. The top speed was measured at 46 mph. (Nov. 28, 1914 *The Daily Journal*)

**1914 American LaFrance** *Ernest C. Richardson III Collection*

**1914 ALF throwing water over the Federal Building** *Ernest C. Richardson III Collection*

**1914 ALF at Middle and Pollock Streets**  *Ernest C. Richardson III Collection*

On December 4, 1914, the Board voted to send the new pumper to the Button Company after a tie vote of 5-5, with the mayor casting the deciding vote in favor of the Buttons. (Dec. 5, 1914 *New Berne Weekly Journal*) One possible reason for going to the Button Company as opposed to the Atlantic was that the Button steamer may have been out of service at this time with mechanical issues.

The New Bern Fire Engine Co. No. 1 headquarters underwent changes in December to make room for the new engine. They moved the horse stall to the back for the hose wagon. (Dec. 4, 1914 *The Daily Journal*)

In late 1914, John Taylor (African American), the driver for the Atlantic Company became ill and could not work. The Board voted to make a donation of $25 to him.

Beginning in December 1914, the city invoked new rules for the 1914 engine. Two engineers were hired to take care of and operate the truck. They paid the first engineer $90 per month, the assistant engineer $50. The truck was not be removed from the firehouse unless one of the engineers was present. Maximum speed limit for the LaFrance on city streets was to be 20 mph. (Dec. 8, 1914 *The Daily Journal*)

Not to be outdone, at a board meeting in January 1915, the Atlantic Steam Fire Engine Co No. 1 petitioned the city for a combination motor driven fire engine. At the same meeting the Riverside Hose Company requested a new brick building be built to house their equipment to take the place of the frame building. (Jan. 8, 1915 *New Berne Weekly Journal*)

The first casualty from the new fire engine occurred on February 9, 1915 when Charles Gibson, a black firefighter, was run over at the corner of Middle and Pollock Street while attempting to jump on the engine as it was responding to a Box 25 alarm. He was thrown beneath the machine with one of the wheels passing over his body. (Feb. 9, 1915 *New Berne Weekly Journal*)

The Atlantics' new American Lafrance engine arrived on April 27, 1915, with identical specifications to the 1914 engine and at a cost of $9000, except it was painted white (their company colors were white and pink). The firemen housed it at their building on Broad Street (owned by T.A. Green). Changes were made to the building including adding a brass sliding pole from the third to first floor and new sleeping quarters. (Apr. 27 1915 *New Bern Weekly Journal*)

On April 30, 1915 a pump test of the new engine produced 800+ GPM. William Ellis, a member of the board of alderman and past chief had his name on the side of the engine, continuing a tradition begun in 1879 by the Atlantics.

**1915 American LaFrance**　　　　　　　　　　　　　　　　　　　　　　　　　　*Ernest C. Richardson III Collection*

Because of a disagreement with the city over operating procedures in May 1915, all Button Company firemen resigned effective June 1, but did not give up their charter. They also gave up their location at City Hall and opted to look for quarters elsewhere. Riverside Hose and Fourth Ward companies petitioned to take their place along with the 1914 engine. (May 14, 1915 *New Bern Weekly Journal*). Cooler heads prevailed and at a meeting on June 1, 1915 with a committee of an alderman and five members of New Bern Steam Company and five from the Atlantic Company. A new set of rules and regulations governing the operation of the fire companies were drawn up. These were presented to the Board of Alderman and the fire companies for approval. (June 8, 1915 *The Concord Daily*). This was approved and the Button firefighters returned to service by the end of the second week in June.

**1914 and 1915 American LaFrances and the Button and Atlantic hose wagons in front of City Hall/Fire Station. Note three bears protruding from the front of the building.**  *New Bern Firemen's Museum Collection*

Fire struck the Norfolk Southern railroad shops on November 16, 1915 completely destroying the shops along with two locomotives and several cars. The fire threatened the northern part of the city including the railroad station and several freight warehouses. Damage was estimated at $200,000. (Nov. 17, 1915 *High Point Enterprise*)

An accident happened on February 28, 1916, as the Atlantic Fire Company's engine was answering an alarm. Garland Eastwood "failed to get his foot on the step of the big machine and was thrown to the ground," as he tried to board the moving engine, reported the *Charlotte Observer* on March 1. Eastwood fell and his head "hit the brick pavement with great force." He suffered a fractured skull and remained unconscious for 336 hours (14 days). His revival "attracted attention in medical circles all over this part of the state" reported the *Raleigh News*

*& Observer* on March 14, 1916. Eastwood, who was a past member of the Fourth Ward Fire Company, was reportedly not a member of any of the companies at the time of the incident. He was left an invalid from the accident and subsequently died in the home of his sister, Mrs. William Styron on North Pasteur Street from complications six years later. He had been "critically ill" for three weeks, reported the *News & Observer* on June 3, 1922 and was buried on June 2.

The January 13, 1917 issue of *The Morning New Bernian* contained a very complete inventory of the Button and Atlantic companies. The detailed description included the amount of old versus new hose, racing hose, couplings, rubber coats and boots, harnesses for the horses, etc.

On March 1, 1917, the city charged two black boys with the theft of brass from the old Atlantic Steamer (Silsby) and selling it to a junk dealer. The steamer was being stored in the vacant Fifth Ward firehouse. (Mar. 2, 1917 *The Morning New Bernian*)

The two steam fire engines were advertised for sale in the March 27, 1917 edition of *The Morning New Bernian*. The Silsby steamer was sold to a former member of the Atlantics.

In June 1917 the Board donated $100 to the Atlantic Company for their planned outing at the seashore later that summer. This was a reward for their service to the city. (June 6, 1917 *The Morning New Bernian*)

The Button Company had a custom which had been carried on for a long time. For value and service to the company, members would receive a watch charm with the name of the company and a picture of the engine on one side, and the receiver's name, length of service and date of presentation on the reverse side. At the banquet on January 3, 1917, members Don Sparrow, LeRoy Tucker and Bob Whitley each received one. (Jan. 6, 1917 *The Morning New Bernian*). The Atlantic Company also issued a token for years of service.

There was a dance for the benefit of the New Bern Fire Company at Ghent Park complete with an orchestra on June 11, 1917, carrying on the tradition of both companies of providing family entertainment for the citizens of the city. (June 8, 1917 *The Morning New Bernian*)

In November 1917, they granted the cemetery committee permission to tear down the old Fifth Ward Reel Hose house as it was in terrible condition. The firehouse was on the grounds of a cemetery in the southwestern portion of the city. (Nov. 4, 1917 *The Morning New Bernian*)

The Benson-Berger Shows appears in Ghent the week of November 5, 1917 under the auspices of the Button Fire Company featuring the Bristol's Society Circus, The Monkey

Speedway, the Palace of Mystery, the Hawaiian Village, Circus Sideshow, the Wild West Show, and the Big Eli Ferris Wheel. (Nov. 2, 1917 *The Morning New Bernian*)

The faithful black Atlantic driver for twenty years, John Taylor, who became ill in 1914, is remembered by the members of the company. He attended more fires than any other individual. (Dec. 25, 1917 *The Morning New Bernian*)

On December 30, 1918 the Hancock Street Christian Church was destroyed when a fire erupted in the basement destroying the wooden structure. Damage was estimated at $7,000. (Dec. 31, 1918 *The Daily Free Press*)

The City appropriated $300 to each fire company for their vacations during a meeting of the aldermen in May 1920. The Atlantic company left in June on a trip to the northern states and Canada. (May 18, 1920 *The New Bern Sun Journal*)

Frank Hammond, the black driver of the Button engine, died suddenly on September 27, 1920 after 25 years of service. Ben Hurst, last of the Button fire company horses, provided the final service carrying his casket to the burial site. (Sep. 28 & 30 *Morning New Bernian*)

The Pine Lumber Company was almost totally destroyed by fire on June 20, 1921 which had a head start before being reported. Thirty-two firefighters under the command of Chief W.J. Disosway responded with the two American LaFrance engines and a hose wagon. Four hydrants were used, however because of low water pressure the engines ended up drafting from the river. The fire burned for 18 hours. Damage was estimated at $98,000. (Sep. 14, 1921 *Fire and Water Engineering*, pg. 514)

Chapter **8**

# Conflagration of 1922

Much of the material for this section is based on an account from F.G. Godfroy, the Superintendent of Water Works in New Bern and the Foreman of the Atlantic Engine Company at the time of the fire, in a paper titled "Water Supply at the New Bern, N.C. Conflagration" published in the July 1924 issue of the *Journal of the American Water Works Association*, Vol. 11, No. 4, pp 904-907.

The morning of Friday, December 1, 1922, the day after Thanksgiving, dawned sunny and warm with an air of excitement filling the area around the train station. Brisk southwest winds were increasing ahead of a cold front across the Ohio Valley. At the train station the high school band was playing as players and spectators boarded a special train bound for Raleigh. The New Bern high school football team was playing Sanborn for the state championship. Temperatures in the low 50s was perfect football weather. Among the 300 passengers were many of the firefighters, members of both the Atlantic and Button companies. It was 7:30 AM as the train left the station. Little did they know what would transpire after they left, in what would become the worst urban conflagration in the history of North Carolina.

Winds continued to increase during the day reaching 50 to 60 mph from the southwest during the afternoon. At 8:38 AM Box 61 was pulled for a fire at the Rowland Lumber Company, Mill #1 on Griffith Street. The mill was owned by the Roper Company, the largest lumber company in North Carolina, but leased to the Rowland Company. During the early 1900s there were no less than 16 lumber mills in and around the city. Most of these mills had fire pumps, some had hose carts, and even one at a small fire department with paid members on duty overnight.

**New Bern train station in the North Carolina County Photographic Collection #P0001, North Carolina Collection Photographic Archives, The Wilson Library, University of North Carolina at Chapel Hill.**

This fire resulted when one of the machine belts became hung-up, creating friction and resulting heat which ignited the sawdust. Fire quickly enveloped the entire saw mill, engine room and dry kilns. Continuous blasting of the mill whistle told employees to evacuate. There were several close calls, and some employees were burned.

New Bern responded with their two American LaFrance pumpers, one a 1914 model, the other a 1915. Two horse-drawn hose wagons filled out the alarm which was the entire firefighting force of the city. Extra hose was brought from the station.

With the lumber yard completely engulfed, they turned their attention to preventing the spread of the fire. Rowland had two 750 GPM pumps, one drafting out of the Neuse River, the other connected to an artesian well. One of the city trucks went to the company pumps, the other tied into the city water mains. The Coast Guard cutter *Pamlico* arrived on the scene and assisted with the firefighting. They brought the fire under control but only after the nearly total destruction of the lumber company. Over a million feet of lumber was destroyed. Firemen were able to save a large storage shed at the south end of the property.

From the rooftop of the Elks building looking northwest.   *Courtesy of the State Archives of North Carolina*

View of the Farris-Nassef Overall factory fire from Pasteur Street.  *New Bern Firemen's Museum Collection*

*New Bern Firemen's Museum Collection*

**Escaping the fire.** *New Bern Firemen's Museum Collection*

About an hour into this fire, Box 32 was struck for a fire at the corner of Queen and Pollock Streets, nearly 1.5 miles from the first fire. The chief responded with two firemen and fire extinguishers in their cars. By the time they arrived, a chimney fire which had ignited the roof of a home had been extinguished by a bucket brigade made up of local citizens.

While at this fire, box alarms 47 and 42 were pulled for fires on Kilmarnock Street. By the time the Chief could free up a hose wagon and engine, fire had spread to over three blocks of buildings. Help was requested from the Kinston and Washington fire departments. Kinston loaded one of their engines with extra hose and made the 35 mile trip over country roads in about 2 hours, arriving at 3:10 PM. Washington loaded their engine onto a railcar and made the trip in 53 minutes, arriving at 3:50 PM. By the time the mutual aid crews arrived, 15 to 20 blocks of buildings were already consumed.

Upon arrival, the Washington engine was assigned to the corner of New and George Street and helped to stop the spread of fire there. Several homes were blown up to create a fire break. The Kinston company was sent to the corner of Broad and Metcalfe Street and helped to stop the spread of the fire there. Again, several homes were dynamited. Six houses were pulled down by a cable attached to a Norfolk and Southern steam engine.

This is one of the first homes dynamited to try to halt the spreading inferno.   *New Bern Firemen's Museum   Collection*

Greenville fire department was asked to respond, but the chief did not want to send his only truck and all the hose out-of-town over the unpaved roads on the windy day leaving the city unprotected.

By 5 PM the wind shifted and threatened the business district. More buildings were dynamited in an effort to create a firebreak, but with gale force winds the fire kept going. All the buildings along Pasteur Street were destroyed. The Dill warehouse was afire. Sparks carried over two blocks set fire to a house behind the Fairview Hospital and near the Coast Line depot. Saint Luke's and New Bern General Hospital were evacuated.

Using other city water supply pumps, pressure was maintained at 20 pounds or greater on the system, even though there were several hundred breaks in the system and hydrants were left open after being abandoned because of the rapid fire spread. The city was furnishing over 5000 GPM on the system. By evening the winds died down allowing the fire to be controlled.

Many of the citizens brought what they could salvage before the fire overran their homes to the Cedar Grove cemetery. There they spent the night guarding their belongings.

Over 1000 buildings were destroyed and 3,530 people were left homeless, many of them African Americans. One fourth of the city lay in ruins. The St. Peter's AME Zion church on Queen St. burned while the nearby St. Cyprian's, the black Episcopal Church, was spared and used as an emergency hospital. The Ebenezer Presbyterian Church and Rue Chapel AME Church lay in ruins. Fire leaped over the train station and destroyed a two and half block area toward the Neuse River. Total damage was estimated at $2,500,000. There was one fatality, a 105-year-old woman, Harriett Reeves, who went back into her house to save a few things and never re-emerged. (Dec. 2, 1922 *The Morning New Bernian*)

Ruins of old Griffin Free School, George Street

New Bern Firemen's Museum Collection

December 2, 1922 edition of The New Bernian

December 2, 1922 Sun Journal

Red Cross assisting at the fire.     *New Bern Firemen's Museum Collection, Photo by Wootten*

Devastation on the north side of town looking toward Cedar Grove Cemetery.     *New Bern Firemen's Museum Collection, Photo by Wootten*

St. Peter's A.M.E.Z. Church, 615 Queen St.　　　*New Bern Firemen's Museum Collection*

The train station was saved as residents and firemen wet-down the roof to prevent fire from taking hold on the structure. Building in the foreground was the Farris-Nassef Overall factory. Photo by Wootten. New Bern Firemen's Museum Collection

Cedar Grove Cemetery in background. *New Bern Firemen's Museum Collection*

**Looking toward West Street School in the distance.** *New Bern Firemen's Museum Collection*

An "insane" black man was initially charged with setting the fire at the Rowland plant. He had escaped from an asylum after being convicted of destroying property belonging to the Rowland Company several weeks earlier, and on the morning of the fire was seen near the plant. He was also a suspect in the fire on Kilmarnock Street and was jailed on evidence provided by the fire chief and deputy fire commissioners. Later investigation would prove both fires were accidental. (Dec. 5, 1922 *The Morning New Bernian*)

**State Fire Marshal Sherwood Brockwell and Fire Chief James Bryan at the location where the second fire started on Kilmarnock Street. Sparks from the chimney ignited the roof and spread to other homes.** *New Bern Firemen's Museum Collection, Photo by Wootten*

The Women's Club of New Bern went door to door raising funds, collecting clothing, bedding and other supplies and also set up a soup kitchen for those that were displaced. Fort Bragg was contacted which responded with eight freight cars loaded with 500 army tents, cots, mattresses, and other necessities and their mobile kitchen which prepared food for the homeless. The naval base at Norfolk sent one thousand cots and blankets and sweaters. Kinston sent three tons of clothes. Even little Cove City shipped a boxcar load of supplies. They raised over $15,000 in a couple of hours. Donations poured in from around the country as the story of the fire was headlined in most newspapers.

Turner-Tolson Furniture, the Episcopal Parish house, the Christian Science Church, Meadows warehouse and the West Street School all opened their doors for the homeless. The Methodist Church provided meals for the white victims and volunteers. Kafer's Bakery and Home Bakery provided loaves of bread, the Swift and Armour Company sent a large quantity of ham, and Sterling Mills shipped a train car load of flour.

The tent city set up near where the Stewart Sanitorium once stood on George Street, took nearly two weeks to construct. Each tent had a wooden floor and walls as well as a wood stove. Each family was given two tents, set up so the doors faced each other. One tent was for cooking, the other for sleeping. The Red Cross provided utensils and other items. This was a temporary home for nearly two years to some, but many people chose to leave New Bern. (Dec. 8, 1922 *The Morning New Bernian*)

The Rowland Company was the main source of employment for the African American community. Nearly five hundred men were employed in the sawmill and another 500 in logging. After the fire, A.R. Turnbull, owner of the Rowland Company, agreed to rebuild the mill if he could negotiate the sale of the plant from the Roper Company. Other lumber companies went on a 24 hour schedule to help meet demand and provide employment for those affected by the Rowland fire. The sale to Rowland was closed on May 6.

The Rev. R.I. Johnson of St. Cyprian's Episcopal Church established the Good Shepherd hospital for the blacks. Blacks could not rebuild their homes on George Street or Cypress Street leading up to Nunn Street. A park was built on George Street and the city expanded the Cedar Grove cemetery.

New fire codes forbid the use of wood shingles in the city which was the main culprit in the rapid spread of the fire.

There was intense excitement and apprehension when a new fire on December 6, 1922 struck about seven blocks from the area devastated by the December 1st fire. The New Bern Collegiate and Industrial Institute school building and a dwelling were destroyed and two nearby homes damaged. Quick work by the fire department and the lack of wind prevented this fire from extending further. (Dec. 6, 1922 *The New Bern Sun Journal*)

View of tent city off of George Street.  Courtesy *Sun Journal*

Two months later, on February 8, 1923, fire struck the Rowland Lumber Company again causing an estimated $40,000 damage to the machine shops and destroying the roof of the building. Much of the machinery was destroyed. (Feb. 8, 1923 *Salisbury Evening Post*)

Oh, by the way, the New Bern high school won the football game 6-0.

December 8, 1922 New Bernian

**Where it all started. Roper plant leased to the Rowland Lumber Company.** *New Bern Firemen's Museum Collection,*
*Photo by Wootten*

# Chapter 9

## 1923-1959

*A portion of the following is from the minutes of the city aldermen.*

On June 15, 1923 fire destroyed the building of the Scott Register Company at the foot of Queen Street. Damage was estimated at $20,000. The Atlantic Coast Lines railroad formerly used the building as a passenger station. (June 15, 1923 *The Progress*)

Once again fire struck an Atlantic Coast Line freight building at the foot of Queen street on November 2, 1924 destroying the structure. The building was built over the water which made firefighting difficult. One engine pumped from the river, the other used a hydrant. Firemen worked for 3 hours to bring the fire under control. The loss was estimated at $30,000. (Nov. 4, 1924 *Morning New Bernian*)

At a June meeting of the aldermen in 1925, $250 was authorized for each company for their summer outing as a reward for their service.

Retiring Chief James Bryan gave a report for 1926 at a January 1927 meeting of the aldermen. Total loss for fires was $47,257.50 (one half of the loss was from the Mill Supply Company fire). There were 111 fire alarms during 1926. James Oglesby was elected Chief of the Button Company, Albert Jowdy became assistant chief of the Atlantic Company. Chief Bryan recommended the purchase of a city service truck (carries ground ladders). (Nov. 28, 1927 *New Bernian*)

Fire destroyed Kafers Bakery on Middle St on April 6, 1927 after flames broke out in the furnace room shortly after 2 am. Around 4 am the Atlantic fire engine broke down. With the fire threatening the Eastern Bank and Trust and the Bangert building, Kinston and Morehead City were called for mutual aid. When Morehead City's engine arrived, it replaced the Atlantic engine at the corner of Middle and Pollock street. Damage was over $50,000. (Apr. 6, 1927 *New Bernian*)

On May 2, 1927 a fire at a small warehouse adjoining the Neuse Motor Company on lower Craven Street around midnight claimed the life of Harry Roberts. Roberts was trapped in the rear of the building where he had living quarters. A cigarette was responsible for the fire. (May 3, 1927 *New Bernian*)

June 1927... Bids opened for a new 1000 GPM engine. American LaFrance bid $12,800, Ahrens Fox $14,350, Mack $14,500, and Seagrave $13,950. Bid awarded to Seagrave.

The new Seagrave city service truck, named after the mayor "Albert H. Bangert", arrives and is pump tested on the dock behind the Gaston hotel on November 26, 1927 (Note: Delivery of the truck in less than five months was exceptional considering that delivery times now are usually over a year). The engine was an "F" style 6 cylinder, 1013 Cubic inches with a 4 stage pump rated at 1000 gallons per minute. It produced over 1300 gallons per minute from a hydrant. Total cost of the new truck was $13,950 cash. (Nov. 28, 1927 *New Bernian*)

**1928 New Bern Fire Department drivers.**   *Courtesy NCSFA*

The new main station on Broad Street opened in 1928. The station would house both the Button and Atlantic Companies in one building. With the goal of saving money on the rental of buildings, the design of the station still showed the differences between the two companies as the building contains two sliding poles, one for each company. There are two stairwells leading to the second floor, one for each company. The second floor is divided in half, one side for the Button, the other for the Atlantic. The sliding poles are hidden from each other by a wall on the second floor.

Fire alarms during 1930 totaled 122.

On February 15, 1931 fire gutted the upstairs room in a 64 Main Street residence from a defective flue killing William Simpson, a seven-year-old invalid. Fire Chief William Smith tried in vain to break into the room and rescue the boy. (Feb. 16, 1931 *Statesville Record and Landmark*)

(Left) Edgar B. Elliott

Firefighter Edgar B. Elliott drowned on June 10, 1931 while fighting a major fire along the Neuse River that destroyed a gasoline launch, two barges, a tugboat, and a storage warehouse. Estimated damage was $200,000. Firefighter Elliott was attempting to save a barge captain although other accounts stated he was attempting to rescue a family trapped on a barge.

Fire on November 27, 1931 destroyed the Brinson Memorial school building at Grantham, three miles toward Morehead City on Highway 70. New Bern responded with an engine, but by the time they arrived the fire had spread from the basement boiler room to the first floor. There were no hydrants and the engine couldn't get close enough to the Neuse River to draft. A futile attempt was made to fight the fire with bucket brigades, but in the end all they could do was watch the building be consumed by the fire. (Nov. 27, 1931 *New Bernian*)

The Old Tabernacle Baptist Church at the corner of Broad and George Streets, built in 1895-97, was destroyed by a 9 pm fire on November 28, 1931. The fire started near a flue in the annex and was visible in all parts of the city as it spread up through the roof and steeple. The loss was estimated at $20,000. (Nov. 28, 1931 *The New Bernian*)

On December 9, 1931 fire destroyed the Belk Brothers Department store and Block's Ready To Wear shortly before 3 am on Middle Street causing $200,000 in damage. The fire began in the three-story annex in a boiler room behind the store and had been burning for some time before being discovered by the night watchman. Firemen prevented the fire from spreading to other structures including the James Hotel. Strong winds fanned the fire, however a steady rain kept the embers from spreading the fire. Morehead City and Kinston responded under mutual aid, but the fire was under control by the time they arrived. A crew from the Coast Guard cutter *Pamlico* assisted at the scene. The 1915 American LaFrance was damaged at the fire. (Dec. 9, 1931 *The New Bernian*)

Fire destroyed the two story Shaw Drug Store building at the corner of Middle and Pollock Streets shortly before 3 am on January 2, 1932. The Central café and Wooten-Moulton photographic studio also occupied the structure. Damage was estimated at $50,000. (Jan. 2, 1932 *The Sun Journal*)

A defective flue was responsible for a fire that destroyed the Turner-Tolson furniture store with a loss estimated at $50,000 on November 17, 1932.

An early morning fire destoyed the Vogue store on January 6, 1933. Smoke and water damage was reported in four other buildings with a total loss of $50,000.

April 16, 1933... New Bern responds mutual aid to the Morehead City waterfront for a fire at the Atlantic Hotel. The 3-story building containing 300 rooms along with the hotel's annex and a building containing several small apartments were destroyed. New Bern sent an engine which was assigned to extinguishing several minor roof fires which had been ignited by sparks some distance from the hotel. (Apr. 17, 1933 *Morehead City Gazette*)

A collision between the Atlantics' 1915 American LaFrance fire truck and a Chevrolet light coach on December 2, 1933 at the intersection of Queen and George Streets in New Bern left one person dead. The crash occurred at high speed as both vehicles were traveling "swiftly", the fire truck answering a fire alarm in Riverside. None of the firemen were injured. (Dec. 1 & 2, 1933 *The Sun Journal*)

The following are from city aldermen meeting minutes (indented portions):

1933....157 fire alarms during the year

June 1940.... Alderman Smith recommends that the oldest fire engine be turned into a fire boat (using the pump and engine from the fire truck).

March 3, 1942.... bought 2500' hose (thru purchase and government contract). Advertise for bids for a 1 ton pickup to carry hose.

August 4, 1942.... Drivers pay increases from $110/month to $125/month

A new pumper arrived in August 1936 manufactured by the W.S. Darley Company of Chicago. The 500 GPM engine, mounted on an International chassis, was delivered at a cost of less than $2500. Named the "Edgar B. Elliott", it was dedicated to the memory of the firefighter who lost his life in 1931.

**Edgar B. Elliott Memorial**

The Banner warehouse and a nearby building were destroyed in a fire May 9, 1938 with an estimated loss of $50,000.

On August 10, 1938, a seventeen foot tall granite memorial in memory of Edgar Elliott was unveiled at Cedar Grove Cemetery in connection with the convention of the North Carolina Firemen's Association being held in New Bern. Fire departments from across the state donated money for the construction of the monument.

(Left) Atlantic Fire Company members who traveled to Cuba in July 1936 for their city-sponsored vacation. Members present include Floyd Paul, "Shorty" Kafer, A.W. Brinson, Mel Rhodes, G.B. Land, W.H. Purrser, Raymond Thompson, Mike Jowdy, Sam Dill, Sam Cook and George Misthy. On the bottom of the picture is written "One Grand and Glorious Time". Firefighters had to meet a minimum number of fires, drills, and meetings in order to be eligible. New Bern Firemen's Museum Collection.

A mutual aid fire in Jacksonville sent the New Bern Fire Department with two engines to the high school on February 15, 1940. Defective wiring was thought to be the cause. High winds fanned the flames and only the gymnasium was saved. Loss was estimated at $90,000. (February 16, 1940 *Wilmington Morning Star*)

New Bern responded with an engine and eight firemen to the business district in Beaufort September 24, 1940 when fire destroyed the Beaufort Hardware, Pender's, and Owens Brothers' Grocery with damage estimated at $50,000.

Chief A.J. Davis reports 148 fire alarms during 1942.

January 5, 1943... Drivers pay raised to $150/month, Chief $50/month, Assistant Chief $25/month

February 2, 1943.... Chiefs pay $75/month

Three teenage sisters died in a two-story house fire on Hancock Street January 25, 1944. The fire was discovered at 2:10 am when Box 16 and then Box 14 were pulled. Fire was blowing out of the upstairs apartment when firemen arrived. Heavy black smoke filled the entire structure. It was the largest loss of life in the city in 75 years. (Jan. 26, 1944 *The Sun Journal*))

February 1, 1944....Three smoke masks purchased.

September 5, 1944.... Chief A.A. Kafer recommended either rebuilding one of the old trucks for $7500 or buying a new one for $9000 OR combining the two old trucks into one serviceable truck. Aldermen recommended advertising for a 750 GPM pumper.

October 3, 1944.... bids received from ALF, Seagrave, Mack. Decision tabled until a report of the cost of rebuilding of one of the old trucks.

November 1944.... cost of rebuilding 1914 truck $1898.50. It was suggested that a 500 GPM pumper would serve the city better. (Read more about this in the *Mystery of the Missing Fire Truck* chapter)

July 6, 1945.... Chief Elzie Bell recommends the purchase of two 750 GPM pumpers, a new fire station in Ghent and one in Riverside. He proposed a fire district for Five Points.

August 7, 1945... Bids opened for a new fire truck. Only one bid received because of tight specifications... American LaFrance at $8375. The new engine would be named "L.C. Lawrence" after the mayor

July 30, 1946... new ALF cost $8375 less 2% for cash on delivery. In August the city passed a resolution to prevent the new truck from leaving the city on fire calls (it took part in parades outside the city)

October 16, 1946... monthly appropriations for Atlantic and Button companies increased to $200/month.

Dec. 3, 1946...5 paid employees receive $180/month.

March 23, 1948... Chief T.I. Davis requested a fire alarm whistle. Granted.

Nov. 16, 1948....3/4 ton pickup for FD. Chevrolet dealer bid $1395.

On April 5, 1950 two sawmills of the Wells-Oats Lumber Company between Cove City and Dover were destroyed in a $100,000 fire. The quick response of the New Bern Fire Department prevented the fire from reaching the dry kiln, planing mills, boiler plant and dry lumber facilities. (Apr. 6, 1950 *Asheville Citizen-Times*)

June 1950... County to purchase one fire engine for rural firefighting and turn over to the city for housing and operation. Two firefighters hired by city @ $2460/yr. (Note: At this time there were no other fire departments in Craven County). New Gamewell fire alarm system purchased for $18,261.89

**Craven County engine**  *Courtesy NCSFA*

An accident on February 26, 1951 left fire truck driver, Robert Broadstreet, Jr., unconscious after the engine overturned while en-route to a grass fire. Broadstreet was pinned under the truck. He suffered a cerebral hemorrhage while in the hospital and remained in a coma. The other three firefighters on the truck, Past Chief A.A. Kafer, Clyde Smith and Tim Connor, were not seriously injured, but were hospitalized. The 1936 International/Darley engine was stripped of its equipment and hauled away to the city yard. (Feb. 27, 1951 *The Sun Journal*). Firefighter Broadstreet passed away on January 5, 1963 from his injuries.

May 15, 1951... Advertised for bids for a 500 GPM truck.

June 1951.... Bids for a new engine received from Darley $6689, Fire Control Equip (John Bean) $9057.10, Mack $9969.95 less a $400 trade allowance, Oren Roanoke $11,520 less $1250 trade in.

July 1951... Bid awarded to Oren Roanoke GMC for $10,250.

On July 24, 1952 at 4:35 pm a raging riverfront fire destroyed three businesses. Destroyed were the Haminton's Café, Wallace Holton's Garage, and the Sanderlin Battery Company. The fire started in the wall between the café and garage. Several explosions kept the firemen at a distance. Cherry Point firemen responded to assist. Damage was estimated at $100,000+. (July 24, 1952 *The Sun Journal*)

April 6, 1954... McCotter lot on National Ave. purchased for substation

May 18, 1954... bid opening for a fire truck. Separate chassis and pumper body bids. Bids from GMC, International, Dodge. Pumper body bids from Oren, Seagrave, John Bean

June 1, 1954... Bid awarded to Flowers Motors (GMC) $4697 plus Fire Control Equipment (John Bean) $10,860.

A raging waterfront fire on the Trent River June 11, 1954 at the foot of Craven Street caused damage in excess of $400,000 to a Montgomery Ward warehouse containing furniture, tires and appliances. Eight 2 ½" hoselines were used to fight the fire. Two firemen were overcome by smoke. The fire was confined to the one structure. The fire scene was the same location where firefighter Edgar Elliott was killed in 1931. (June 12, 1954 *The Sun Journal*)

Sep. 7, 1954.... Bids for radio equipment: Motorola $5036.63 and GE $5040.00). Bid awarded to Motorola. Fire station construction bids ranged from $13,252 to $17,996.

Jan. 4, 1955... report on the safety of Ghent fire station.

March 31, 1955... Mutual aid to Atlantic Beach for a fire that destroyed the Ocean King Hotel and three other buildings including the police station. Damage estimated at $400,000.

**July 18, 1955 New Bern Fire Department**  **Courtesy NCSFA**

At about 1 am on October 21, 1955, a fire at the foot of Hancock Street near the Trent River destroyed the freight warehouse of the Atlantic and East Carolina Railway which also housed two beer distributing companies. A switch engine operator discovered the fire on a track near the building. The loss totaled $200,000. Long-time residents said this was the third warehouse to burn at this location. (Oct. 21, 1955 *The Sun Journal*)

Fire swept through the 30-room Neuse Forest Convalescent home causing $50,000 in damage late in the afternoon on December 9, 1955. Twenty-one elderly and infirmed residents were moved to safety. Firemen had trouble getting a good water supply as their source for drafting out of was shallow. (Dec. 10, 1955 *The Sun Journal*)

    May 1, 1956.... looking into a rescue truck (county would pay half)

    Nov. 6, 1956.... only 36 of 110 fire alarm boxes installed.

July 26, 1957... city asked to be reimbursed $15,000/year from county for maintaining and operating the county truck with paid drivers. County balked at this arrangement. City voted to return the truck to the county and not respond outside city limits effective 7/31/1957. They would provide mutual aid when requested.

August 3, 1957... city requested from the county $1250/month to maintain and provide drivers for the county's rural pumper (county took no action)

September 16, 1957.... ordinance established for the retirement policy for firemen.

January 2, 1959... Motorola awarded a contract for base station and 20 home monitors.

## Chapter 10

## 1960-1999

*This chapter is in the form of a timeline with notes from the aldermen meetings.*

Gale force winds hindered firemen battling a fire in two waterfront downtown buildings on February 11, 1960. Flying embers touched off other fires as far as nine blocks away. Several million gallons of water from hydrants and the Trent River were poured onto the structures. It took 10 hours to bring under control. The walls of the building housing the Ace Electric Company, Ubanks' Refrigeration Service and a furniture store warehouse collapsed. Firemen from Cherry Point, Kinston, Washington, Greenville, Vanceboro and Bridgeton aided New Bern. Damage was estimated at $150,000 to $200,000. (Feb. 11, 1960 *The High Point Enterprise*)

Fire destroyed the Commodore Boat Works at about 6:20 am on March 24, 1960. Several partially built boats along with lumber and machinery and the paint division were destroyed at a loss of $500,000. (March 24, 1960 *Gastonia Gazette*)

Kinston's worst fire in 65 years occurred on Christmas day in 1960 destroying the Sutton Building with four stores on the first floor. There was damage to an adjoining department store and furniture company. New Bern responded mutual aid. Damage was estimated at $500,000. (Dec. 26, 1960 *Rocky Mount Telegram*)

From the minutes of the city aldermen (indented portions):

> July 24, 1961.... proposed ordinance for fire department. Fire Chief appointed by aldermen, Paid Captain appointed by City Manager

September 5, 1961... North Carolina Fire Insurance Rating Office recommends appointing fire chief for an indefinite period.

September 26, 1961... Mutual aid to Radio Island, Beaufort when the USNS Potomac exploded and burned while docked. The 600 foot tanker was unloading 8.5 million gallons of aviation fuel and high octane gasoline. The fire threatened much of the waterfront including several storage tanks. Fire departments from as far away as 200 miles responded. (Sep. 28, 1961 *Statesville Record And Landmark*)

October 4, 1961... city ordinance... Chief serves for 3 years, option for 3 more. Volunteer companies objected to this stating that members, not the city should elect the chief.

July 1962... city adopts fire prevention code.

August 1962... Rescue squad organized.

May 1963.... bids for an 85' ladder: Seagrave $40,934.22, w/optional equip. $49,378.47; American LaFrance $45,527.72, w/optional equip. $53,448.42. Contract awarded to Seagrave w/optional equipment $44,415.62.

A fire on January 5, 1963 at around 12:30 pm destroyed the Virginia-Carolina Chemical plant on Airport Road at the Trent River near the location of the Highway 70 bridge. Strong winds ignited grass and brush fires which crossed the highway. Township 7 and New Bern firefighters were on the scene. (Jan. 5, 1963 *The Sun Journal*)

July 1963.... Township 7 purchases county truck from New Bern for $3198.00.

September 3, 1963... bids for pumper. Seagrave $29,667.25, Howe $28,795.78. Contract awarded to Seagrave.

January 19, 1964.... New Seagrave 85 foot aerial arrives at 1:30 pm. The city ordered the truck May 21, 1963 at a cost of $44,535.62. Powered by a Waukesha gas engine the truck is named after Dr. Dale T. Millns. The ladder truck replaced the 1927 Seagrave (in its thirty-seventh year of service!) which was held in reserve. (Jan. 20 1964 *Sun Journal*)

**1963 Seagrave 85 foot aerial.**  *Albert Brinson Jr. Collection*

February 1964....1000 GPM Seagrave pumper delivered.

    February 12, 1964... city caves on a 3-year term for Fire Chief and reverts to 1-year term with the members electing the chief (the ordinance proposed in 1961 never took effect)

    April 1965... dispatching system to be installed at New Bern Broad Street station.

On November 2, 1965 at about 1 am the 110-year-old Governor Tryon Hotel was destroyed by a suspicious fire along with several businesses in the building. Damage was estimated at $1 million. Also destroyed were an A & P store, photo studio, hardware store, bakery, loan company, and other offices. Firemen from Kinston, Cherry Point, Vanceboro, Bridgeton and Township 7 assisted with 100 men and 11 pieces of equipment. The Tryon was formerly known as the Gaston Hotel. (Nov. 2, 1965 *The Daily Times-News)*

**Governor Tryon Hotel** *New Bern Firemen's Museum Collection*

*New Bern Firemen's Museum Collection*

*New Bern Firemen's Museum Collection*

*New Bern Firemen's Museum Collection*

*New Bern Firemen's Museum Collection*

A two-alarm fire on March 8, 1967 left 11 persons homeless after destroying 2 adjoining homes. One firefighter suffered facial burns. Firefighters struggled for 4 hours to save the rest of the block.

Strong winds fanned a fire at the Arant Lumber Company on April 22, 1967 which began around 6:30 am. The three alarm fire on North Craven Street was fully involved upon the arrival of firemen manning six trucks. Flames were shooting 40 to 60 feet high. Fortunately, the winds were blowing the flames toward the Neuse River so no other structures were threatened. Damage was estimated at $250,000. It was the second fire at the facility in three days. The earlier fire did $500 damage to a green lumber sorting rack. (Apr. 22, 1967 *The Sun Journal*)

**1927 Seagrave city service truck operating at the Arant lumber company fire.** *Albert Brinson Jr. Collection*

A five-alarm fire destroyed the main sawmill of the Scott Lumber Company on Airport Road, shortly before 8 pm on May 26, 1967. Damage was estimated at $200,000. Hundreds of spectators who rushed to the scene to observe the massive fire hampered firefighters. Township 7, New Bern and Bridgeton firefighters fought the blaze. Between the two lumber company fires in a month's time, the ability of the city to produce lumber was nearly eliminated. (May 28, 1967 *The Sun Journal*)

A twin-engine light airplane crashed and burned shortly after takeoff from the New Bern Airport on June 21, 1968 at around 4:40 am. Prominent Raleigh engineer William Olsen Jr. was killed. (June 22, 1968 *The Daily Times-News*)

> November 19, 1968... bid openings for a new engine. Ward LaFrance on a Ford chassis $31,412.62, on International $32,548.87; John Bean on a Ford $36,984.40, on an International $37,284.41. Contract awarded to WLF on Ford (lease-purchase arrangement)

On March 2, 1969 two classroom buildings of the West Street Elementary School were destroyed by fire which began around 6 am Sunday morning. Arson was suspected as three simultaneous fires developed in the two buildings. Firemen from New Bern, Bridgeton, Cherry Point and Township 7 fought the fire. Parents had protested the previous week about the unsanitary and overall conditions of the buildings in the predominately black school which was built in 1918. Damage was estimated at $250,000. (Mar. 3, 1969 *The Sun Journal*)

Fire destroyed twenty-three yachts at the New Bern Yacht Club on March 29, 1969 around 2 am. Most of the docks were also destroyed. New Bern responded mutual aid to assist West of New Bern fire department. Damage was estimated at $500,000. (Mar. 29, 1969 *The Sun Journal*)

> New fire station proposed at the old water treatment plant on Highway 70 (never built).

On January 24, 1970 eight families were left homeless after fire destroyed the Hughes apartment building, on Craven Street near Queen. The red brick building was formerly the Craven County Hospital. Damage was estimated at $125,000. (Jan. 25, 1970 *The Sun Journal*)

Hughes apartment building fire.

*NBF&R Collection   Photographer Unknown*

February 1970... the fire department presented the need to the board for two (2) 1000 GPM pumpers to replace the 1933 and 1946 trucks.

September 1971... bids on a new pumper received: American LaFrance Pioneer Custom $41,825.13, on a Ford $39,893.19; Howe on a Ford $39,094.32, w/optional CMH pump $36,584.24, w/optional CPK pump $37,247.19; Ward LaFrance on a Ford $38,241, Ward LaFrance Ambassador and Caterpillar diesel $41,283, w/6V-53N Detroit $41,502, w/6-71N Detroit $42,678. Contract awarded to Ward LaFrance on Ford.

October 1973... GMC pickup received for fire department to use as a "hose wagon".

On January 17, 1973 at around 3 pm, fire gutted the vacant Coca-Cola building near the foot of Middle Street. The upper floor was fully involved when firefighters arrived. The building was slated for demolition.

**Coca-Cola building fire January 17, 1973.**   *NBF&R Collection Photographer Unknown*

ALDERMEN:
JACK R. CRAWFORD
L. R. MORGAN
TIM A. MONTGOMERY
TOM I. DAVIS
GRAHAM D. BIZZELL

CECIL KING
MAYOR
J. C. OUTLAW
CITY MANAGER
H. E. RUSSELL
CITY CLERK & TREASURER

City of New Bern
FOUNDED 1710
P. O. BOX 1129
New Bern, N. C. 28560

# Proclamation

I, the undersigned, do hereby decree that Monday, March 12, 1973 be proclaimed Albert W. Brinson Day throughout the City of New Bern in commemoration of his invaluable and time-consuming services toward the fire department of the City of New Bern, North Carolina.

## Albert W. Brinson -- Fireman

Joined Atlantic Steam Fire Engine Co. No. 1 Oct. 6, 1919. Has served 53 years 4 months active service.

Elected as secretary of company Dec. 7, 1925 and has served continuously for 48 years.

Elected as Atlantic member of Fire Board Dec. 2, 1929. Served 5 years. Served as secretary of Fire Board from Jan. 10, 1964 through Feb. 5, 1973.

Elected as Atlantic member of Firemen's Relief Fund Board Dec. 2, 1940 through Feb. 5, 1973, 33 years. Elected as secretary-treasurer of the Relief Fund March 11, 1968, served until Feb. 6, 1973, 5 years. Made honorary life member and secretary-treasurer emeritus by the New Bern Firemen's Relief Fund Board Feb. 6, 1973.

Elected as Atlantic Pension Fund secretary-treasurer Jan. 6, 1958, serving continuously to the present time.

Appointed to N. C. State Firemen's Association Executive Committee 1938 and served continuously through 1963.

Elected as N. C. State Firemen's Association statistician in 1940. Served through 1963 — 23 years.

N. C. State Firemen's Association plaque presented to him in 1958 for distinguished service as statistician.

N. C. State Firemen's Association plaque for dedicated service rendered in Pension Fund legislative programs 1960.

Presented Atlantic Steam Fire Engine Co. No. 1 plaque for 50 years 5 months active dedicated service and 45 years secretary, 1970.

Elected to an active life membership by Atlantic Steam Fire Engine Co. No. 1 Dec. 6, 1965.

Firemen's statue presented to him by 25-Year Club of the N. C. State Firemen's Association in 1968.

Member of N. C. State Firemen's Association 1919-1973.

Each year of his membership in the Atlantic Company he has made the required percentage of alarms entitling him to the free annual trip.

Albert W. Brinson was appointed from the Atlantic Fire Company as a member of the original Firemen's Museum Committee and was elected as secretary-treasurer of the New Bern Firemen's Museum Committee on October 7, 1955 at the organizational meeting, which position he has held continuously to the present time.

This eighth day of March, 1973.

Cecil King
Mayor, City of New Bern

**March 23, 1973 was declared as Albert W. Brinson day in New Bern.**

Fire completely destroyed the Coplon-Smith store at 232 Middle Street on September 4, 1974 in a late-night blaze which took five hours to bring under control. This was the oldest and at one time the largest department store in town. Thick smoke prevented the firemen from finding the source of the fire. Shortly after midnight flames broke through the roof. Volunteer companies from Bridgeton, Tri-Community, West of New Bern, Little Swift Creek and Townships 7 and 9 were called to assist. Firewalls prevented the spread of the fire. However, there was extensive smoke damage to stores on either side. (Sep. 5, 1974 *Sun Journal*)

**February 22, 1975**  NBF&R Collection  Photographer Unknown

Shortly before 4 am on February 22, 1975 fire broke out at 207 Middle Street and spread to seven interconnected stores. Stores destroyed included a clothing store, a television repair shop, Army-Navy surplus store, clothing store, LaMarick Beauty Salon, Liberty Loan shop, Friendly Wig shop and the New Bern Bible and Book Store. The fire spread from Middle Street to Tryon Palace Drive. Mutual aid assistance received from Township 7 and West of

New Bern. A broken gas line which caused several explosions worsened the fire. Three firemen suffered minor injuries. (Feb. 22, 1975 *The Sun Journal*)

**Middle Street, February 22, 1975**

*NBF&R Collection  Photographer Unknown*

**February 22, 1975**  NBF&R Collection  Photographer Unknown

On February 22, 1976 fire destroyed the Dixie fertilizer plant. Strong winds blew possibly hazardous ammonia smoke across the Neuse River forcing the evacuation of 160 Bridgeton residents. Lightning is believed to be the cause of the fire which did an estimated $2 million in damage. (Feb. 23, 1976 *The Sun Journal*)

1976... Elizabeth Avenue fire station built.

Fire did heavy damage to the New Bern Academy on September 21, 1977, the state's oldest school building. The blaze started in the attic. Dating from 1764, the school burned down in the late 1700s and was rebuilt in 1806. (Sep. 22, 1977 *The Daily Times-News*)

October 1977.... Bids opened on diesel powered 1000 GPM engine with a high pressure booster pump. Pierce $70,139.00, Ward LaFrance $71,049.50, FMC $68,947.85. Contract awarded to Pierce.

October 1982... Bids opened for a 1000 GPM pumper. Bids: ALF $99,936, Quality $102,090, Atlas $103,027.49, Pierce $111,882.50. Contract awarded to Quality.

Title of fire captain changed to Station Chief in July 1983. The paid Station Chief was responsible for supervising the paid personnel, administer personnel policies, and be in charge of all equipment and records.

April, 1984…Bids opened for 1000 GPM/ 1000 gal tank, diesel pumper. Bids: Jack Slagle $119,287, American LaFrance $113,655. Bid awarded to American LaFrance.

One third of MacDonald Junior High School was destroyed by an arson fire that started around 2:40 pm on June 5, 1985. Damage was estimated at one million dollars. The fire began in the teachers' office on the second floor and spread into the tar roof and over the classrooms. Three firefighters suffered minor injuries. New Bern was aided by nine fire companies from Craven County. A 13-year-old girl was charged with setting the fire. (June 6 *Sun Journal* & June 13, 1985 *Asheville Citizen-Times*)

September, 1986…Bids received for a 1000 GPM pumper/500 gallon tank. Bids: American Eagle $122,446, Pierce $110,732, Zimmerman-Evans $109,734, Triad $110,088, Carolina $110,475. Bid awarded to Zimmerman-Evans (Quality).

May 1987... About 130 city fire alarm boxes for sale after the department began taking down the system on May 1. (May 3, 1987 *Sun Journal*)

April 15, 1987... delivery of $109,000 Ford fire pumper from Quality Manufacturing. Named the "Ella Bengel"

On June 23, 1987 a New Bern fireman was injured in a blast at the Damco Inc. building, 1219 Pollock Street when he was hit by a gallon can. Sparks from a welding torch ignited combustibles. (June 23, 1987 *Sun Journal*)

September 1987.... first female firefighter joined the ranks of the volunteers.

A fire at the Mission Rest Home on Dillahunt Road around 12:27 am on July 30, 1989 led to the death of one 78-year-old resident and sent 15 others to the hospital. West of New Bern fire department assisted at the scene. Damage was estimated at $75,000. (July 31, 1989 *The*

*Sun Journal)*

An explosion and fire at the Hatteras Yacht Company, a builder of luxury yachts, killed one person and sent 40 others to the hospital January 4, 1991. The fire broke out in the research and development area at about 7:15 am. A hazardous materials unit from the Cherry Point Marine Corps Air Station was called to the scene. (Jan. 5, 1991 *Asheville Citizen-Times*)

An arson fire at the Palace Motel in December 1991 resulted in $350,000 in damage. The fire occurred in the early morning hours in a vacant room on the east front wing. The federal Alcohol, Tobacco and Firearms (ATF) agency was called in to investigate.

On July 4, 1993 an arson fire gutted the old Trailways bus station on Broad Street. The fire had two points of origin. Seven county fire departments assisted New Bern. (July 4, 1993 *Sun Journal)*

Fire gutted the Durham Furniture Store, 4005 Hwy 17 South around 9:30 am on May 18, 1994. Strippers, lacquers and other chemicals fueled the fire. New Bern received mutual aid from Rhems and West of New Bern. (May 18, 1994 *Sun Journal)*

June 1994.... Zodiac Hurricane H560 fireboat purchased for $42,500.

May 1995... Dispute between New Bern's volunteer firefighters and the paid staff over a city proposal to increase the paid staff by 30%. The Station Chief asked for 9 additional firefighters. The volunteer Fire Chief disagreed. For generations the volunteers had been putting out the fires while the paid staff had charge over maintenance and getting the trucks and equipment to the scene. (May 16, 1995 *Sun Journal)*

An afternoon fire on April 29, 1997 destroyed the B & R bowling alley on Tatum Drive requiring mutual aid from every fire department in Craven County. The fire was aided by combustible chemicals stored inside for maintaining the lanes. Damage was estimated at $500,000. (Apr. 30, 1997 *Sun Journal)*

Ground was broken for the new main station on Neuse Boulevard October 14, 1998.

On December 2, 1999, what every firefighter dreads, fire struck New Bern's Elizabeth Street fire station causing significant damage to the roof. The fire started when a stove was left on as firefighters responded to what turned out to be a false alarm. (December 8, 1999 *Sun Journal)* The station was remodeled in 2008, adding 1200 square feet (for a total of 4700 sq. ft.) at a cost of $530,000.

## Chapter 11

# 2000-Present

*Minutes from City aldermen meetings are on indented portions.*

On May 3, 2000 two men perished in an early morning fire in what was supposed to be a condemned and boarded-up house on the corner of Cypress and Cool Streets. (May 4, 2000 *Sun Journal*)

An early morning fire on July 17, 2000 destroyed Lane's Barbecue House on Route 17. Mutual aid from West of New Bern and Rhems. (July 18, 2000 *Sun Journal*)

November 18, 2000... dedication of new 27,000 square feet main station on Neuse Blvd. Fire department moves to 800 MHz for communications around the time of the opening of the new station.

On July 18, 2001 fire safety robot "Pluggie" unveiled at the New Bern Fire Station on Neuse Boulevard. The fire safety robot came to the department via the efforts of the Berne Village Retirement and Assisted Living Center which raised the funds.

> September 27, 2001.... groundbreaking for Thurman Road fire station #2. Dormitories for 9 firefighters. The station would total 4100 square feet at a cost of $460,000.

An early morning fire on January 21, 2002 gutted Applebee's Neighborhood Grill on Route 17. The 4:15 am fire started in an office near the kitchen. Mutual aid received from West of New Bern and Township 7. (Jan. 22, 2002 *Sun Journal*)

On October 8, 2002, 56 residents of the Magnolia Place retirement home at 3407 Oaks Road were evacuated as heavy smoke and fire erupted from the east wing. No one was injured. An investigation determined that the fire was set. An arrest was made two days later. (Oct. 9,

2002 *Sun Journal*)

June 2004.... Zodiac Hurricane H560 fireboat purchased for $42,500.

October 2004... new four-story fire training tower and burn building off of Renny's Creek Drive completed.

March 2005... New Bern Fire and Rescue upgraded to medium rescue capabilities (requires a minimum number of personnel certified in rescue techniques, a minimum amount of rescue equipment, and a vehicle for transport of the equipment and personnel)

February 2006.... City achieves a Class 3 fire rating. This routine inspection is required on a regular basis as part of the North Carolina Response Rating System (NCRRS). The inspection evaluates communities on nationally recognized standards including emergency communications, needed fire flows, water supply, community risk reduction, and the equipment, staffing, training and operation of the fire department. A fire district's rating can range from 1 to 10 with 1 being the best and 10 being the worst. The higher rating (Class 1 is the highest) may lead to lower insurance rates for citizens and businesses of the fire district.

March 2006.... new Boston Whaler 25' Guardian Grade series fireboat purchased at a cost of $126,500. Marine 1.

October 2006... one million dollar grant from Dept. Of Homeland Security allows New Bern to hire 12 additional firefighters. Now 21 fire fighters/shift vs. 12/shift. Total FF 63.

December 2006.... Sutphen 75' quint purchased at a cost of $563,000.

**Marine 1**  *Photo by Andrew Bartholf*

On May 18, 2007 at 5:45 pm a major downtown blaze erupts after a spark at Smitty's Welding Shop on Queen Street starts a fire that spread to the Blessed Hope Church on Pollock Street. Mutual aid received from Little Swift Creek, Township 7, West of New Bern, Tri-Community and Rhems fire departments. (May 19, 2007 *Sun Journal*)

November 2007....68 paid New Bern fire fighters

March 2012... Fire Chief Aster asks the city for more firefighters and two more stations to properly protect the city. They need this to maintain the city's Class 3 rating and minimize response times.

An old 6000 square foot warehouse at 901 North Craven Street which was originally part of the Atlantic and North Carolina Railroad dating back to the 1850s was destroyed in a suspicious fire on May 28, 2012. The building was being rented to Precision Molding. This was also the site of the 1909 fire at the railroad shops.

**May 28, 2012 fire at the old railroad warehouse.** *Courtesy Gary Hollar Photography*

On June 18, 2014 fire destroyed a large part of the Cooper's Landing apartment complex on Simmons Street. At least 8 apartments were destroyed. Mutual aid received from Little Swift Creek, West of New Bern, and Township 7 fire departments. (June 19, 2014 *Sun Journal*)

August 1, 2014.... delivery of new Sutphen 75' quint. Named "Lee W. Bettis Jr". Cost $756,633.

Fire destroyed the Lynaire Kennels on Old Cherry Point Road on May 19, 2016. Twenty-five dogs and several cats succumbed. New Bern received mutual aid from Township 7, Township 6, Havelock, West of New Bern and Tri-Community fire departments.

On January 12, 2017 an afternoon fire at the Trent Villas condominiums destroyed several apartments. Mutual aid from Township 7. (Jan. 13, 2017 *Sun Journal*)

In one of the largest fires in recent memory, a fire at around 4 am on January 17, 2018 destroyed the RA Jeffreys beer distribution center on Red Robin Lane. It took 2 hours to bring the fire under control. Mutual aid from West of New Bern, Township 7, Tri-Community, Little Swift Creek and Rhems. (Jan. 18, 2018 *The Sun Journal*)

R A Jeffreys fire January 27, 2018.    *Courtesy Tradewind Aviation International*

In early March 2019 the New Bern Fire Department announced that a recent state inspection and audit of New Bern Fire-Rescue performed by the North Carolina Department of Insurance resulted in a Class 2 rating for the community. Previously, New Bern was listed as a Class 3 community. New Bern's new Class 2 rating puts it in the top 2% of fire districts nationwide. In North Carolina, New Bern now ranks as one of the top 28 fire districts out of 1,533 total.

# Chapter 12

# Conventions & Tournaments In The 1880s Through Early 1900s

*Description of the early contests from the 1916 Proceedings of the North Carolina State Firemen's Association.*

In the 1880s through the early 1900s, competition was a way for firefighters not only to hone their skills, but also a way to maintain their interest in the fire service. In past years it was hard to sustain fire companies as the lack of fire responses led to apathy among the personnel, which often resulted in the companies disbanding. There is no greater example than the period of the 1700s and early 1800s in New Bern when fire companies did not last. The steamers and hose wagons led to not only competition among fire companies in the city, but also with other cities across North Carolina.

Steamer competition included both standing quick steam and running quick steam. In the standing quick steam, the steamer started with a cold boiler. The steamer would draw water from a cistern or river. Upon a starting signal, the firemen would fire up the boiler using wood soaked in a combustible material. The time was taken when the boiler produced enough steam to operate the pump and throw a stream of water. In the running steam, the steamer would race a distance, disconnect the horse team pulling the steamer, and then throw a stream of water after placing the hard suction in a source of water.

For the hose wagon races, the wagon would start with 288 feet of 2 ½" hose. A firefighter would stand on the back step of the wagon. There was a driver. The firefighter on the back step would hold the coupling end of the hose along with a few folds of extra hose. Upon a signal, the horse and wagon would cross a line and race to a hydrant. Without stopping, the firefighter on the back step would jump off and wrap the hydrant with the hose. The wagon would continue laying out the balance of the hose. After the wagon had gone a short distance, the backstep firefighter would attach the hose to the hydrant. Reaching the end of the hose, the driver would attach the nozzle, signal the other firefighter to turn on the hydrant and flow water. The time was taken when a stream was thrown.

Other competitions included the hose reel races, both short and long distance. Up to 16 firefighters pulled the reel. The team raced 150 yards to the hydrant and then played out at least 98 feet of hose on the reel. The hose would be uncoupled from the balance of the hose on the reel, a nozzle attached and water flowed. Grab reel races were timed distance races by a crew running 50 yards to the reel, pulling a hose reel another 50 yards, unreeling not less than 48 feet of hose, attaching to a hydrant and throwing water.

New Bern did not take part in the hook and ladder contests or the horse hose reel race.

The New Bern companies, including the independents, were very successful in the competitions, accumulating many trophies and cash prizes. From 1895 to the early 1900s, both the Button and Atlantic companies had junior firemen who took part in some tournaments.

When the teams returned home from competitions in other cities, they were usually met at the train station by a large crowd of enthusiastic supporters and a brass band.

Below are some of the competitions the department attended and results. You will note that the white companies held separate tournaments from the black companies. The black conventions were markedly different from those of the whites. There was a much more religious overtone to their proceedings with most sessions opening to a singing of praises to the Lord. A "Committee of Thanks" praised the local citizens for opening up their homes and feeding the visiting firemen.

In addition to the usual firefighters competitions, the black conventions included individual competitions such as the 100 yard dash, sack race, barrel race, potato race (two contestants were entered from each team...one at a time they would run to a location where 10 potatoes were lined up, pick one up and race back to the start with the next teammate repeating the process until all 10 potatoes were picked up) and baseball games.

In May 1875, the New Bern Steam Fire Engine Co. attended a tournament in Charlotte with their Amoskeag steamer as part of that city's centennial celebration. In appreciation of the hospitality shown by the Charlotte firefighters to the New Bern contingent, New Bern one year later sent three 2 ½ x 3 foot framed pictures of the Amoskeag surrounded by photographs of the members of the company to the Hornet, Pioneer and Independent fire companies of Charlotte. Over the group in gilded letters appeared "Centennial Greeting" and under it "Charlotte 1775-1875". (May 20, 1876 *Charlotte Observer*)

It was a custom of the New Bern squads over the years to send a card of thanks to the host cities in which they took part for their friendship and support.

July 1885... New Bern Steam Fire Engine Company participated with their steamer in Wilmington. In competition with two Wilmington steamers, the Adrian and Little Giant, they won the two quick steaming events. For the wins they received prizes of a silver pitcher which swung on pivots, a goblet and a large brass clock. Upon returning to New Bern they were met at the train station by the Atlantic Steam Engine Company, the Mechanics Hook and Ladder, the Silver Cornet Band and over fifteen hundred enthusiastic fans. (July 18, 1885 *The Daily Journal*)

**Framed picture sent to Charlotte.**

July 12, 1887... Competition between the Silsby and Button steam engines at the foot of Craven Street. In the first water contest, flowing water through a 50' hoseline and across a 50' line, the Silsby won in 2 minutes, 52 seconds. New Bern's time was 3 minutes, 33 seconds. In the afternoon contest, flowing water through a 100' hoseline, the Silsby won in 4 minutes, 20 seconds and Button's time was 4 minutes, 24 seconds. The last test was filling a bucket suspended 60' in the air. The Silsby won with a time of 51 seconds with the Button at 2 minutes, 28 seconds. Fireworks followed at 9 pm. (July 13, 1887 *The Daily Journal*)

July 12-14, 1892... North Carolina State Firemen's tournament in Asheville. The Atlantic Company sent their Silsby which won first prize in the quick steaming competition as there was no competitors. (July 9, 1892 *The Daily Journal*)

August 31, 1894...The Atlantic Company won first prize in the quick steaming competition in Salem with a time of 3 minutes and 15 seconds.

**Atlantic Company posing in front of the Main Hall building of Salem Academy after winning the quick steaming competition in 1894.** *New Bern Firemen's Museum Collection*

August 6-9, 1895... North Carolina Firemen's Convention in New Bern. Many businesses in town were closed on the last day of the convention as the city "turned out en masse to do honor to the firemen." Competition teams from Greenville (4 companies), Wilmington, Raleigh, Fayetteville, Greensboro, Winston, Salem, Monroe, Salisbury, Durham, New Bern and more. New Bern sent an engine to Wilmington so they could send two steamers to the tournament. (July 20, 1895 *The Daily Journal*)

**Five steamers near Union Point Park pumping from the Neuse River at the 1895 Convention in New Bern.**  *New Bern Firemen's Museum Collection*

(Right) 1895 Convention Ribbon

**Hook and Ladder in front of the old City Hall during the 1895 convention parade.**  *New Bern Firemen's Museum Collection*

October 12, 1895... The Atlantic Company hose reel team composed of 14 Atlantic and four Button members won second prize at the World's Fair in Atlanta, losing out to New York City. They competed against 52 fire departments, five nations, and 47 states. The Atlantics were crowned the "champion of the South".

Members of the team: Ellis Williams (A), William Clark (A), Herbert Simpson (A), Dave Foy (A), Jim Gaskill (A), Willie McCarthy, Captain (A), Herbert Willis (B), Fred Richardson (A), Albert Bangert (B), Jim Delemar (A), Claud B. Foy (A), H.M. Roberts (A), George Roberts (A), John Timberlake (A), Joe Congdon (B), John Matthews (A), Tom Daniels (B), Fred Thomas (A).

**This tournament actually took place in 1896.** *New Bern Firemen's Museum Collection*

The Atlantics took their steamer and hose reel to the North Carolina Association tournament in Salisbury August 19-21, 1896 and came away with first prize and the championship belt in the reel contest, and two second place prizes and a third in other contests. (Aug. 23, 1896 *The Daily Journal*).

The Atlantics' Silsby Steamer won the quick steaming competition at the 9th annual convention of the North Carolina Firemen's convention in Fayetteville August 3, 1897. The New Berne Button was a close second. (Aug. 6, 1897 *The Daily Journal*)

**Atlantic team circa 1900.** Courtesy *State Archives of North Carolina*

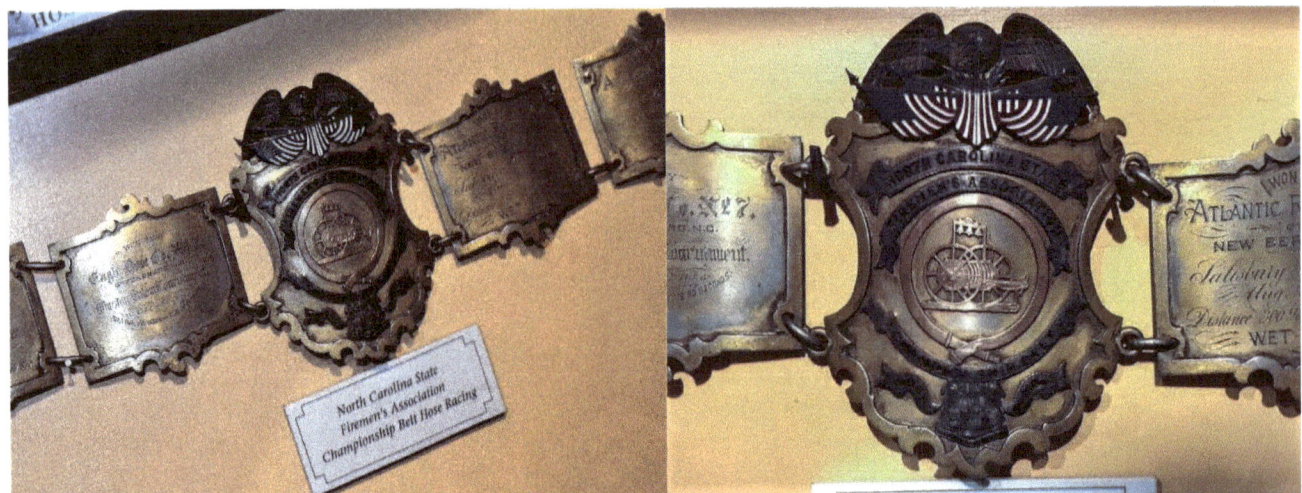

NC State Fireman's Assoc. (NCSFA) Hose Reel Championship Belt
*Mike Legeros photo*

*Displayed at the Greensboro Historical Museum.*

Atlantic Reel Team wins in Salisbury (1896) and Fayetteville (1897). *Displayed at the Greensboro Historical Museum, Mike Legeros photo*

**1899 Atlantic reel team composed of Atlantic and Button members in Wilmington.** *New Bern Firemen's Museum Collection*

July 12-13, 1900... Button steamer won the standing quick steam in world record time of 1 minute, 46 4/5 seconds at Wilmington. The Button also set a world's record of 2 minutes, in the running quick steam competition. This was the last year for the running quick steam because of the expense of shipping horses to the contests. In the junior competition, the Atlantic Juniors won the hand reel contest when 3 other teams had their hose blow off the hydrant. (July 12, 1900 *The Daily Journal*)

**New Bern reel team practicing on Pollock St.** *New Bern Firemen's Museum Collection*

**Atlantic hose wagon at competition in 1900** *New Bern Firemen's Museum Collection*

August 1, 1904... Twenty firemen from the Button and Atlantic companies traveled to Salisbury along with a large group of fans for the state tournament with the 2 steam engines and a hose wagon. In the contest, the Button's tinder was soaked in an extremely combustible substance. When the firebox was lit, the steamer jumped a foot off the ground. The judges were bewildered as they had just given the rig a thorough inspection and had found nothing that might disqualify them. (Aug. 2, 1904 *New Berne Weekly Journal*)

So, what was the secret to the success of the quick steaming by the boys from New Bern. They used what is known as light wood, a pine which burns hotter and is easier to light. Next, they filled a condom with ether which is very volatile and highly flammable. When this was thrown into the firebox, it exploded into flames which quickly brought the steamer up to operating pressure, often in under two minutes.

July 19, 1905...Atlantic Steam came in second with a time of 3 minutes 17 3/5 seconds in the quick steaming competition in Winston-Salem and first prize in the distance contest. (July 20, 1905 *The Raleigh Morning Post*)

August 1907... At a competition in Wilmington, the Button steamer did not perform up to par, taking over four minutes to build up steam. The engineer, upon cleaning the engine, found a burlap bag stuffed in the suction inlet. The perpetrator was never uncovered. (Aug. 13, 1907 *New Berne Weekly Journal*)

**Button hose wagon set a world record of 27 seconds at 1908 competition in Wilmington.** *New Bern Firemen's Museum Collection.*

August 19, 1909...20th annual convention of the North Carolina Association of Colored Firemen met at New Bern. Firemen from 26 cities attended the conference. Hose wagon races, a hook and ladder contest, and a parade were part of the festivities which included a business meeting. The parade consisted of 25 companies and nearly 500 men in varied uniforms, decorated floats and young ladies singing various anthems. Many of the visiting firemen had to appeal to the public in their hometowns for funds to attend the convention. In addition, accommodations had to be found for the firemen as local hotels refused to house the black firefighters. Fifty dollars was appropriated by the city board for entertainment. (Aug. 25, 1909 *East Carolina News*, Kenansville)

The 1910 North Carolina State Firemen's Tournament was held at New Bern the week of July 25-30 in conjunction with the city's bi-centennial celebration. Spencer set a world record of

17 seconds in the 100 yard grab reel contest. Salisbury won the 150 yard hand reel race in 24 2/5 seconds. Kinston won the horse hose wagon race in 29 seconds. (July 30, 1910 *The Daily Press,* Newport News)

**Unidentified reel team on George Street in New Bern during 1910 convention.** *Courtesy New Bern Historical Society*

**Asheville hose wagon in competition at the Ghent fairgrounds in 1910** *Courtesy New Bern Historical Society*

**Sanford hose wagon in competition at the Ghent fairgrounds in 1910** *Courtesy New Bern Historical Society*

**Atlantic Junior reel team in 1910.**  *New Bern Firemen's Museum Collection*

September 12, 1910... The Sixth Ward Reel Company came in second in the grab reel race in 23 seconds and came in first in the hose wagon race in 35 seconds at competition in Winston for black firefighters. (Sep. 13, 1910 *New Berne Weekly Journal*)

May 16, 1911...Ten men from the Button Company, their hose wagon and horse plus 15 men from the Atlantic Company, their steamer, hose wagon and horses attended the state firemen's tournament in Charlotte. The Button Company won the hose wagon race in a world record time of 26 2/5 seconds. (May 16, 1911 *New Berne Weekly Journal*) Note: There is some question about this being the world record. According to Chief S.G. Bernard of the Asheville

Fire Department and the records of the North Carolina State Firemen's Association, the Asheville team was 1/5 of a second better in 1909. The Association for an unknown reason changed the times after 1915 to 26 1/3 seconds for Asheville No. 1 in 1909 and 26 ½ seconds by New Bern No. 1 in 1911. The mystery deepens when we see that these two times were the only ones changed over time. At state sanctioned events there was usually three timekeepers. The official time was the agreed upon time between the timekeepers. (June 2, 1911 *New Berne Weekly Journal*, 1915 & 1940 N.C. State Firemen's Assoc. Proceedings)

**Button hose wagon after winning in 1911** *New Bern Firemen's Museum Collection*

Official scoreboard May 19, 1911 hose wagon race. James D. McNeil, President of the North Carolina Firemen's Assoc (left), Chief Orr of Charlotte on right.
*Courtesy New Bern Firemen's Museum, Photo by Andrew Bartholf*

**Ben Hurst with driver Frank Hammond**  *New Bern Firemen's Museum Collection*

**Button and Atlantic teams July 17, 1911** *New Bern Firemen's Museum Collection*

August 1911... Sixth Ward Hose Company wins first prize in the long-distance reel race at the North Carolina Black Firemen's Tournament in Elizabeth City with a time of 26 seconds. They also came away with first prize in the grab reel race with a time of 23 seconds and first prize in the hose wagon race with a time of 27.5 seconds. (Aug. 18, 1911 *New Berne Weekly Journal*)

July 24-25, 1912.... At the state firemen's tournament in Fayetteville, the Button Company won the state hose wagon race on Wednesday and on Thursday the Fourth Ward Company split second, third and fourth money with two Raleigh teams and Riverside took fifth prize. The Button and Atlantic companies were disqualified on Thursday when their hoses blew off the hydrant. A large crowd of people met the returning teams at the train depot. (July 27, 1912 *The Daily Journal*)

**Atlantic reel team in Fayetteville (1912). Front row: Eugene Williams, Sam Coward, Ben Williams, Will Dowdy, Fred Thomas. Back Row: Joe Nelson, Mathew Hall, Tom H. Smith. Ladies were unidentified.** *New Bern Firemen's Museum Collection.*

August 13-14, 1913.... At the firemen's tournament in Wilmington, Riverside won the hose wagon race with a time of 30 seconds, the Button Company was second with 30 3/5 seconds, the Atlantic Company was third with 31 1/5 seconds and the Fourth Ward won fifth prize with a time of 33 1/5 seconds. Several companies lost when their hose blew off the hydrant because of strong hydrant pressure. (Aug. 14, 1913 *The Daily Journal*)

October 31, 1913... At the East Carolina Fair in New Bern, the Riverside Company won the hose wagon race in 35 2/5 seconds with Morehead City taking second place at 36 1/4 seconds. The local companies raced for time leaving the prize money for the visiting teams. (Nov. 1, 1913 *The Daily Journal*)

**Glenburnie fairgrounds July 4, 1913**  *New Bern Firemen's Museum Collection*

August 5, 1914... Four New Bern hose wagons (Atlantic, Button, Riverside and Fourth Ward) attended the tournament in Winston-Salem. New Bern and Riverside tied for second with a time of 31 3/5 seconds. (Aug. 6, 1914 *The Daily Journal*)

September 7, 1914.... In a city hose wagon race Riverside came in first with 37 1/5 seconds. The Atlantic Company on their second attempt (the timer did not get a time on the first run) clocked at 38 2/5 seconds. The Button Company was disqualified when the hose blew off the hydrant. Fourth Ward logged 40 ½ seconds. The companies sponsored the Liberty Shows Carnival Company in conjunction with their competition to raise money for the 1915 tournament in New Bern. (Sep. 8, 1914 *The Daily Journal*)

Where the Great Eastern Carolina Fair and New Bern "Home Coming" Festivals are Held.

Ghent Fairgrounds where much of the competition took place in New Bern. Also, the Atlantic and Button companies would bring the circus to town here and hold dances in the casino. *Ernest C. Richardson III Collection.*

East Kinston team at the 1915 tournament on Spencer Ave. led by "Brack" the beer drinking horse. During races this horse had to be started blindfolded. *New Bern Firemen's Museum Collection*

**Kinston team 1 during 1915 convention parade on Middle Street.** *New Bern Firemen's Museum Collection*

Motorized vehicles and expenses brought an end to this type of competition. However, other contests were devised over the years. During the forty-first annual convention held in New Bern in 1928, there was the usual truck and reel races, but also outdoor motor boat races and free-for-all boat races. There was also a beauty contest, firemen's ball, street dancing and a large parade with floats. (Aug. 2, 1928 *The Nashville Graphic*)

In another form of competition, the first baseball game played at Kafer Park on George Street in 1928 featured the New Bern Battery D Team against the New Bern Fire Department.

Retired Atlantic steamer and hose wagon at August 11, 1938 convention parade in New Bern.   *New Bern Firemen's Museum Collection*

**1938 Convention Parade.**  New Bern Firemen's Museum Collection

Many fire departments in the area have held firemen's competition days. In 2000, New Bern hosted such a competition during the Chrysanthemum Festival. Four events were scheduled: hose lay, dump tank draft, tower rescue and the bucket brigade. In the hose lay competition, four firefighters each unroll a 1 ½" hose, couple the hose together, attach a nozzle, connect to a pumper and throw water at a target. For the dump tank event, four firefighters lay on cots "asleep". At the sound of an alarm they get up and dress in their turnout gear, drive the pumper to a tank, drop suction hose in the tank and using a handline shoot water at a target. The tower rescue requires a four-person team to rescue a person atop a tower. They must raise a ladder, two firefighters climb the ladder, "rescue" the person and bring the victim down the ladder, where the other two firefighters will carry the victim on a stretcher 20 feet to the finish line. For the bucket brigade, eight person teams fill a 55 gallon drum on a platform with a water shuttle.

# Chapter 13

# The Horses

Ben Hurst, Fred, Old Jim, Dick and Prince are but a few of the legendary horses to serve with the New Bern Fire Department. Most times, especially in the 1880s through the early portion of the twentieth century, they performed other functions within the city such as road work and garbage pickup.

Before the arrival of the first steamer, most of the equipment was hand drawn. When the Amoskeag steamer was delivered in 1865, it was originally pulled by hand. Weighing in at 6000 pounds, the steamer would have required many men to pull it. It didn't take long for the steamer to be converted to horse-drawn, and so began the era of the horses.

Before the purchase of horses by the city in 1880 and after the Amoskeag was converted to horse-drawn, the following resolution was adopted by the city. Any person that arrived at the firehouse of the steam engine on an alarm of fire with a horse that could pull the steamer would receive $5.00. The owner of the second horse to arrive and used to pull the steamer would receive $2.50. (June 9, 1874 *The New Berne Times*)

In 1879 the Silsby steamer was purchased. Elijah Ellis, a prominent member of the community and longtime member of the Atlantic Company, donated two horses to pull the steamer. (Apr. 26, 1879 *The Newbernian*)

The first fire horses were purchased in 1880, named Dick and Prince. "Old" Jim was purchased in 1882. He would serve the longest time of any horse, into the early 1900s. A February 17, 1903 issue of the *New Berne Weekly Journal* said "Why not retire poor, old Jim. The veteran horse has served the department for over 20 years but now is in an exhausted condition". Old Jim died at 34.

**Old Jim**                                                      *New Bern Firemen's Museum Collection*

An October 9, 1883 *The Daily Journal* article had the following observation. The newspaper was next to the Atlantic Fire Company and when the fire bell rang for an alarm of fire. The horses rushed from their stalls when they were opened and took position under the drop harnesses even without direction, since the driver was absent.

On January 19, 1894, two new full blooded Percheron horses arrived for the Atlantic Company. A colt, Barry, was purchased for the Atlantic Company in 1902. The Atlantics' "old" horse was then put on duty with the Rough and Ready Hook and Ladder Co. This company could now attend all fires. (Apr. 4, 1902 *New Berne Weekly Journal*)

An article appeared in the Nov. 29, 1907 *New Berne Weekly Journal* about one of the horses that pulled a hose wagon. On a fire call on Cedar Street the horse balked at leaving the station. "Imagine, if you can, the absurdity of having a horse that is a confirmed balker for a fire horse… he never did get to the fire and every means that could be devised, for an hour, failed to move him." Fortunately, the fire was not serious.

Fred was purchased in 1908 for the Atlantic Company. Ben Hurst followed in 1910 for the Button Company along with "Johnny" for the Fourth Ward Hose Company. The Riverside horse was named "Callie", purchased in 1911.

Ben Hurst, last of the Button Company horses, carried the casket of his black driver with 25 years of service, Frank Hammond, to his burial site in 1920. (Sep. 28 & 30, 1920 *Morning New Bernian*)

Fred and Ben were still in service when the Great Fire of 1922 occurred, pulling the two hose wagons to the fire. Fred died in 1925 at 25 of a heart attack on the way to what turned out to be a false alarm. The ironic nature of this is that his driver of all those years, Jon Taylor, also died of a heart attack one week earlier.

With the advent of motorized vehicles, the era of the horse came to a close by the mid-1920s, however, Fred still resides at the Museum!

# Chapter 14

## The Mystery of the Missing Fire Truck!

*Much of the following is taken from the minutes of the city aldermen on file at the city clerk's office.*

There's been a bizarre rumor floating around for many years that a fire truck was either taken apart or buried in whole or in part beneath the floor of the Broad Street fire station. As the story goes, the firemen were upset with the city since they desperately needed a new truck to replace one of the older ones in the aging fleet. They thought by "losing" a truck they would force the city to buy a new engine. There is a discolored area in the flooring at the rear of the station which currently houses the Firemen's Museum, which at one time was a mechanical pit for servicing the trucks. Some firemen claimed they saw white parts in the pit (the 1915 American LaFrance was white and had been involved in an accident on December 2, 1933 when a driver ran into it, so there may well have been white parts in the pit).

So how did this rumor get started? This story is just as interesting. In 1944 the Chief and the city looked into rebuilding either the 1914 or 1915 American LaFrance engines which were still in service. Keep in mind, this was during World War II and the needs of the military severely limited the ability to get a new truck. In fact, unless there was a defense plant or military installation in your city, there was no chance of receiving new fire apparatus and fire department supplies. Many of the fire truck manufacturers had converted their plants to making not only military fire trucks, but also vehicles and parts for the Army. American LaFrance was also making airplane parts, and Mack was constructing 6 x 6 army trucks.

City officials went to the W.S. Darley Company, a well-known family-owned fire truck manufacturer in the Midwest, for their opinion on rebuilding one of the old engines. Basically, the company told them it was not a good idea. Both trucks were 30 years old, had chemical tanks, right-hand drive, a less than adequate chassis and outdated rotary gear pumps. A new truck would only cost a little more than a conversion.

**Discolored area where the mechanics pit once was.** *Photo by Andrew Bartholf*

Not satisfied with that answer, the mayor asked the city mechanic to estimate the cost of rebuilding one truck using parts from the other. The mechanics estimate was $1898.50 for the "vintage" rebuild. Not happy with the estimate, the city advertised for a new 750 GPM pumper.

But what to do with the 2 old engines. They decided to keep the 1914 ALF, putting new tires on the vehicle. The 1915, which had an accident and mechanical issues over the years, was to be advertised for sale. They received two bids, one for $150, the other $200. The alderman rejected these bids and re-advertised the truck for a minimum bid of $250. No bids were received. They made a decision to junk the truck and use the parts as needed. They left the truck outside **behind** the station.

A junk dealer came along 5 months later and inquired about the truck, noting that he could use some of the parts. The city approved the purchase of the parts by the dealer for $11!

But what happened to the rest of the 1915 fire truck is unknown. Was it cut up or buried in whole in the fire station? With its string of bad luck, including an accident which led to the death of a fireman in 1916, breaking down at a fire in 1927, being damaged at a fire in 1931, and the accident in 1933, the firemen may have wanted to get rid of the jinxed truck. The mechanics pit was filled in in the 1950s so that a kitchen could be installed. There are no firemen around from that era to corroborate the story. We may never know what happened.

As a footnote to this story, the 1914 truck remained in service into the late 1940s.

Chapter **15**

# New Bern Firemen's Museum

*Photo by Andrew Bartholf*

The original museum was housed in a building on Hancock Street behind the Broad Street fire station. At an aldermen meeting on June 7, 1955, aldermen Boyd and Richardson suggested that the fire department should sell its surplus ladders and apply the proceeds to the restoration of two old horse-drawn engines (Silsby and Button). The city approved the first budget for the museum in June 1956.

Fortunately, the city was able to re-acquire the two steamers as they were sold at auction in 1917. The hose cart used by the Union soldiers during the Civil War was found in Tarboro, NC and returned. Other equipment, including the two hose wagons of the Atlantic and Button companies and the 1914 American LaFrance engine were also found and returned.

On June 24th, 1957 there was a dedication of the museum with the ambassador to Switzerland, H. De Torrente, on hand along with Congressman Graham A. Barden. Mayor Mack L. Lupton cut the ribbon admitting the guests into the museum. A dinner followed at the Hotel Governor Tryon at which the ambassador presented a flag of Switzerland and trophies from the Berne Switzerland fire department, a gift from the president of Berne, and unveiled a portrait of Baron de Graffenreid, the founder of New Bern, NC. Albert W. Brinson, secretary-treasurer of the Firemen's Museum accepted the gifts. (From the New Bern Firemen's Museum 1957 dedication book

(L-R) Chairman L.R. Tucker, Museum Secretary-Treasurer Albert W. Brinson, Swiss Attache Van Muyden, New Bern Mayor Mack L. Lupton, Swiss Ambassador H. de Torrente, Marine Corps Air Station Cherry Point Lt. Gen. Munn. *New Bern Firemen's Museum Collection*.

**Original New Bern Firemen's Museum**  *Photo by Andrew Bartholf*

In 1999 a new fire station was built to replace the Broad Street station. With the old station vacant, discussions took place about moving the now crowded museum into the vacated fire station. It was sorely needed as the museum building was in a state where major repairs were needed.

Several times the museum came under pressure to remain open when budget cuts threatened its survival. Through fund raisers and generous donations, the museum was able to stay open.

After nearly a million dollars in renovation to the Broad Street station, the "new" museum opened in 2016. A formal dedication took place on December 1, 2017.

*New Bern Firemen's Museum Collection*

**Dedication of "No Burn" Bear on May 18, 2019**　　　　　　　　　　　　　　　　**Photo by Author**

Dedication on December 1, 2017

*Courtesy Robert Manning*

**Former Station 1 now the New Bern Firemen's Museum** *Photo by Andrew Bartholf*

The impressive collection at the museum contains the Silsby and Button steamers, two hose wagons from the 1890s, a 1914 American LaFrance engine, and a 1927 Seagrave city service truck. On the second floor is an area dedicated to the 1922 "Great" Fire. Numerous vintage photographs are on display throughout the museum. A kids area can keep them occupied for hours dressing up as a firefighter or playing with Thomas the Train.

Several things that would be nice to have in the museum we are looking for include: one of the numerous hand pumpers the fire companies had over the years, the dress uniforms from the late 1800s and early 1900s, photographs of fire companies, and anything else related to the history of the department. It's hard to know where these items might be found as evidenced by the following letter which was in Vancouver, Washington near Portland, Oregon!

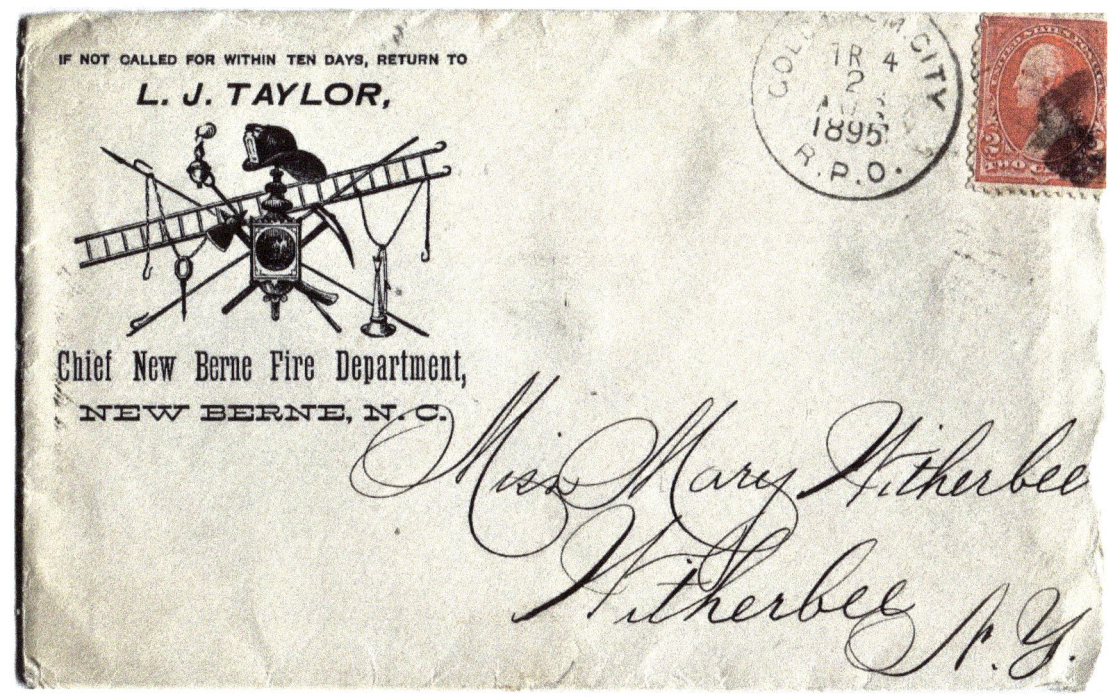

Letter from Chief of Department L.J. Taylor in 1895 found on eBay in 2018… located in Vancouver, Washington. Note the elaborate handwriting to a lady in Witherbee in northern New York.

Check the museum website for hours of operation…**newbernfiremensmuseum.com**.

# Appendix A

# History Of New Bern Fire Companies

| | |
|---|---|
| 1794 | "Water engine" but no organized fire company |
| 1798 | Fire Companies assisted by the militia (act of NC General Assembly) and night watch. There is no evidence that companies were formed as required by this Act |
| 1815-1817 | Three fire companies organized, one for each engine. |
| 1821-1823 | Fire Companies (unorganized, lasted less than 2 years) |
| 1828-1837 | Fire Co. #1,2,3 plus Volunteer Co 4 |
| 1845- Pres. | Atlantic Hook & Ladder Co #1 (Inc 1847), name changed to Atlantic Steam Fire Engine Co. No. 1 in 1887 |
| 1845-1861 | Neuse Fire Co. #2 (Inc 1847) |
| 1853-1860 | Union Fire Co. #3 |
| 1857 | Relief Fire Company No. 2 |
| 1861 | Mechanics Fire Co. #2 |
| 1862-1863 | New York Fire Engine Co. #1 of New Berne |
| 1863 | John Decker Engine Co. #1 |
| 1863-1864 | Denny Bucket & Axe Co. |
| 1863-1865 | Foster Hose Co., Lady Washington Hook & Ladder Co |
| 1864-1873 | Holden Hook & Ladder Co. (Inc 1868) |
| 1865 | Palmer Steam Fire Engine Co.....received Amoskeag Steamer April, 1865...became New Bern Steam Fire Engine Co. #1 |
| 1865-Pres. | New Bern Steam Fire Engine Co. 1 (Inc 1867)…also known as the Button Company |
| 1865-1869 | Harland Co & Kimball Co (merged to become Reliance in 1869) |
| 1867 | New Berne Steam Fire Engine Co., Atlantic Engine Co., Holden Hook & Ladder Co. consolidated to form the Fire Dept of the City of New Bern. |
| 1869-1890 | Reliance Bucket and Axe Company #1 (Inc)...also known as the Independent Colored Company. |
| 1871-1895 | Excelsior Bucket & Axe Fire Co. #4 Inc |
| 1873-1892 | Holden Hook & Ladder Co. #1 becomes the Mechanics Hook & Ladder Co. #1 |
| 1873-1901 | Rough & Ready Hook & Ladder Fire Co. (black) |
| 1887-1888 | Ellis Hose Co. |
| 1894-1900 | Fourth Ward (black) Reel Co. |
| 1894-1911 | Fifth Ward Fire Co. |
| 1898-1912 | Sixth Ward (black) Hose Co. |
| 1910-1917 | Fourth Ward Fire Co. |
| 1911-1917 | Riverside Hose Co. |

Note: From 1895 to the early 1900s, both the Atlantic and Button companies had junior firefighters that participated in some of the tournaments.

# Appendix B

## Chief Engineers of New Bern Fire Dept.

| | | | |
|---|---|---|---|
| 1862 | William Racey | 1887 | Joe K. Willis (Atlantic) |
| 1862-64 | J.W. Denny | 1888 | Ed Pavie (Button) |
| 1864 | Lieut. W.C. Hunt (Army) | 1889 | William Ellis (Atlantic) |
| 1864 | George W. Nason Jr. (Foster) | 1890 | William Ellis (Atlantic) |
| 1864-66 | William Ferrett | 1891 | Ed Pavie (Button)* |
| 1867-68 | Samuel Radcliff (NBSFE) | 1891 | Thomas A. Green* (Atlantic) |
| 1869 | Wm. George Brinson (Atlantic) | 1892 | E.K. Bishop (Atlantic) |
| 1870 | Samuel Radcliff (NBSFE) | 1893 | E.W. Smallwood (Button) |
| 1871 | John S. Manix (Holden) | 1894 | W.D. Barrington (Atlantic) |
| 1872 | I.E. West (NBSFE) | 1895 | L.J. Taylor (Button) |
| 1873 | Samuel Radcliff (NBSFE) | 1896 | W.D. Barrington (Atlantic) |
| 1874 | Thomas A. Green (Atlantic) | 1897 | L.J. Taylor (Button) |
| 1875 | Samuel Radcliff (NBSFE) | 1898 | T.D. Carraway (Atlantic) |
| 1876 | R. Berry (NBSFE) | 1899 | A.E. Hibard (Button) |
| 1877 | Sam. K. Eaton (NBSFE) | | |
| 1878 | Samuel Radcliff (NBSFE) | | |
| 1879 | L.L. Lewis (NBSFE) | | |
| 1880 | Ed Pavie (NBSFE) | | |
| 1881 | R.H. Hilton (NBSFE) | | |
| 1882-84 | James Moore (NBSFE) | | |
| 1885 | William Ellis (Atlantic) | | |
| 1886 | Ed Pavie (Button) | | |

*Ed Pavie died while serving as Chief in 1891.
Thomas A. Green became the acting Chief.

# Appendix C

## Chiefs 1900-Present

| | | | | |
|---|---|---|---|---|
| 1900 | W.F. Richardson (Atlantic) | | 1920 | W.F. Dowdy (Atlantic) |
| 1901 | L.A. Taylor (Button) | | 1921 | W.J. Disoway (Button) |
| 1902 | J.G. De la Mar (Atlantic) | | 1922 | J.B. Bryan (Atlantic) |
| 1903 | Tom Daniels (Button) | | 1923 | C.H. Dixon (Button) |
| 1904 | H.E. Royal (Atlantic) | | 1924 | O.H. Street (Atlantic) |
| 1905 | L.A. Taylor (Button) | | 1925 | W.M. Pugh (Button) |
| 1906 | James B. Dawson (Atlantic) | | 1926 | J.B. Bryan (Atlantic) |
| 1907 | D.M. Styron (Button) | | 1927 | J.W. Oglesby (Button) |
| 1908 | E.F. Richardson (Atlantic) | | 1928 | A.W. Jowdy (Atlantic) |
| 1909 | D.M. Styron (Button) | | 1929 | C.D. Bartlins (Button) |
| 1910 | E.F. Richardson (Atantic) | | 1930 | T.G. Mathews (Atlantic) |
| 1911 | G. Harrington (Button) | | 1931 | W.J. Smith (Button) |
| 1912 | M.L. Hall (Atlantic) | | 1932 | A.A. Kafer Jr. (Atlantic) |
| 1913 | T.D. Davis (Button) | | 1933 | J.B. Simpson (Button) |
| 1914 | T.Y. Lassiter (Atlantic) | | 1934 | J.D. Whitford Jr. (Atlantic) |
| 1915 | T.D. Davis (Button) | | 1935 | E.H. Whitty (Button) |
| 1916 | Sam H. Coward (Atlantic) | | 1936 | V.M. Rhodes (Atlantic) |
| 1917 | E.S. Mitchell (Button) | | 1937 | G.W. Register (Button) |
| 1918 | J.C. Parsons (Atlantic) | | 1938 | Sam L. Dill III (Atlantic) |
| 1919 | R.C. Whitley (Button) | | 1939 | R.W. Ipack (Button) |

1940 S.T. Cook (Atlantic)
1941 M.S. Bray (Button)
1942 Zeb Davis (Atlantic)
1943 J.E. Slater (Button)
1944 A.A. Kafer Jr. (Atlantic)
1945 E.M. Ball (Button)
1946 M.R. Smith (Atlantic)
1947 R.L. Joyner (Button)
1948 Tom L. Davis (Atlantic)
1949 R.G. Broadstreet (Button)
1950 Charles A. Nelson (Atlantic)
1951 Jack Lee (Button)
1952 C. Cyril Edwards Sr. (Atlantic)
1953 X.O. Patterson (Button)
1954 R. Clyde Smith (Atlantic)
1955 Albert Stocks (Button)
1956 Walter Gaskins (Atlantic)
1957 R.M. Whitley (Button)
1958 Joe H. Rice (Atlantic)
1959 J.D. Reece (Button)
1960 C. Cyril Edwards Jr. (Atlantic)
1961 Earl Peterson (Button)
1962 F.H. Phillips (Atlantic)
1963 F.H. Phillips (Atlantic)
1964 Josh Rowe (Button)
1965 J. Vance Lewis (Atlantic)
1966 Preston Carawan (Button)
1967 Albert W. Brinson Jr (Atlantic)
1968 Marvin Cowell (Button)
1969 George Soltow (Atlantic)
1970 W.O. Ernul (Button)
1971 George T. Bowden Jr. (Atlantic)
1972 J. Vic Stanley (Button)
1973 Dallas Waters (Atlantic)
1974 Jacob Jones (Button)
1975 Edward T. Moore (Atlantic)
1976 R.B. Weatherington (Button)
1977 John Whitford IV (Atlantic)
1978 R.B. Weatherington (Button)
1979 Patrick Wynne (Atlantic)
1980 J. Vic Stanley (Button)
1981 George Brinson Jr. (Atlantic)
1982 J. Vic Stanley (Button)
1983 Douglas Soltow (Atlantic)

1984 Reid Whitford (Atlantic)
1985 Allen Broome (Button)
1986 Richard Blythe (Atlantic)
1987 Ralph Gaskins (Button)
1988 David Gray (Atlantic)
1989 Allen Broome (Button)
1990 Warren Taylor (Atlantic)
1991 Eddie Banks (Button)
1992 Steve Allison (Atlantic)
1993 Larry Mares (Button)
1994 Richard Blythe (Atlantic)
1995 Ken Highsmith (Button)
1996 Reid Whitford (Atlantic)
1997 Ralph Gaskins (Button)
1998 Richard Blythe (Atlantic)
1999 Mike Whitfield (Button)
2000 Warren Taylor (Atlantic)
2001 Ronnie Weems (Button)
2002-2015 Bobby Aster
2015-Present Robert Boyd (Button)

# Appendix D

## A Snapshot in Time of What the Firefighting Force Looked Like

1885-1913 from the Sanborn fire insurance maps. The Sanborn map collection consists of a uniform series of large-scale maps, dating from 1867 to the present depicting the commercial, industrial, and residential sections of some twelve thousand cities and towns in the United States, Canada, and Mexico.

|  |  |
|---|---|
| 1829 | 3 hand pumpers, 1 garage was on George Street |
| 1864 | Lady Washington firehouse, Craven St. Near NC Times office |
| 1869 | Reliance Company, Metcalf St. |
| 1871 | Excelsiors, Lane Bldg on Middle St. adjoining the Holden firehouse. |
| 1885 | New Bern station, 41 Middle St, Atlantic station 228 Craven St City Hall. 2 Steamers, 7 hand pumpers, 2 hook & ladder trucks, 1 chemical engine |
| 1888 | 2 Steamers, 2 hose carriages, 2 hook & ladder trucks, 2 independent hose carts, 158 men, 6 horses, 3 men and 3 horses on duty all night at each engine HQ |
| 1893 | Same as 1888 plus 60 fire hydrants |
| 1898 | 160 men, 2 paid drivers always on duty, 3 men and 3 horses on duty at engine HQ city hall all night, 2 hose carriages, 1 hook & ladder, 6 hand reels |
| 1904 | 60 men, 4 paid-2 always on duty, 3 horses always on duty, 2 steamers, 2 hose wagons, 1 hook & ladder, 1 black company with hand reel, 20 Gamewell boxes, alarm bells at City Hall, A & NC Railroad Depot and Five Points. 80 pounds pressure on water system |
| 1908 | Central Station 40-47 Craven St.- 2 volunteer companies, 30 members each, 6 paid drivers on constant duty, 2 paid engineers, 6 horses (also for street work), 2 steamers, 2 hose wagons, 1 hook & ladder |
| | George Street station - 1 black company, 40 members, 1 paid driver on constant duty, 1 horse, 1 hose wagon, 1 hose reel |
| | Gamewell - 20 break glass boxes, 3 alarm station (one at each station and one at Five Points). 5000' 2 ½" hose, 98 hydrants w/pressure of 90 pounds. |
| | Mills-Campbell Lumber Co in James City had 4 paid firemen on night duty. |
| 1913 | 11 paid men, 4 fire companies |
| | New Bern, Craven St. - 5 paid men, 28 men, 3 horses (1 horse alternated between New Bern and Atlantic stations), 1 steam engine, 1 hose wagon w/1200' 2 ½" hose, 1 hook & ladder truck, 1200' 2 ½" hose in reserve |
| | Atlantic, Broad St. - 2 paid men, 35 men, 1 horse, 1 steamer, 1 hose wagon w/1200' 2 ½" |

hose

Fourth Ward, 141 Broad St., between Fleet and Bern - 2 paid men, 25 men, 1 horse, 1 hose wagon w/1200' 2 ½" hose

Riverside, Cypress and George St. - 2 paid men, 23 men, 1 hose wagon w/1200' 2 ½" hose, 1 horse

All horses do street work. 20 Gamewell boxes, 5 alarm stations (1 at each station plus Five Points), 107 fire hydrants, 4 quadruple fire hydrants, fire pressure 90 pounds.

1955    Broad St. Station...1927 Seagrave City Service, 1934 American LaFrance 1000 GPM pumper, 1946 American LaFrance 750 GPM engine, 1951 Dodge/John Bean high pressure fog pumper.
Station 2 Ghent...1951 GMC/Oren 750 GPM pumper,.
Station 3 Riverside...1954 GMC/John Bean 750 GPM pumper.
12 paid firefighters

*New Bern Firemen's Museum Collection*

| | |
|---|---|
| 1969 | 1969 Ford Ward LaFrance w/1000 GPM pump, 500 gal tank at Fort Totten station, 1963 Seagrave 1000 GPM w/500 tank at Broad St., 1963 Seagrave ladder at Broad St., 1954 GMC John Bean 750 GPM 500 tank at National Drive, 1951 GMC Oren 500 GPM, 500 tank at Broad St, 1946 ALF 750 GPM/160 gallon tank at Broad St, 1934 |

*New Bern Firemen's Museum Collection*

ALF 1000 GPM, 160 tank at Broad St, 1 Hi-Ex Foam Generator 5000 CFM. Active Membership 85. Paid Firefighters 17. New station proposed at old water treatment plant on Highway 70.

| | |
|---|---|
| 1985 | Active membership 65. Paid firefighters 30 |
| 2018 | Station 1: 1 Sutphen Engine, 1 Sutphen 100+ Platform, 1 International Rescue, 1 Boston Whaler boat, 1 Zodiac boat, 1 NC State Hazmat tractor trailer<br>Station 2: 1 Sutphen Quint, 1 reserve Sutphen Engine<br>Station 3: 1 Sutphen Quint (this engine is undergoing repair after being damaged in Hurricane Florence), 1 reserve Sutphen Engine<br>Paid firefighters 71<br>Volunteer firefighters: 4 |

**Station 1, Neuse Boulevard.** *Photo by Andrew Bartholf*

# Appendix E

## 1875 New Bern Steam Fire Engine Co. No. 1

The names of the 28 members are (unfortunately I can't place them with a face): Samuel Eaton, Foreman; James W. Moore, Ass't Foreman; E.S. Wormell; Isaac Patterson, Secretary; Master Eddie West; Joseph Schwerin, Treasurer; Giles W. Young; George E. Tinker; Robert C. Keboe; Richard Hilton, Engineer; J. Thomas Mathews; William Salter; A.M. Kirkland; J. Edwin West; Thomas Bowers; A. Zaug; William Lorch; O. Hubbs; E. Hubbs; Samuel Radcliff; Henry G. Russell; James Manwell; George W. Claypole; P.M. Draney; E.M. Pavie, Representative; Richard Barry, Engineer; Walter G. West, Representative; F.D. Schlachter. *All photographs in this appendix from the New Bern Firemen's Museum collection.*

# Appendix F

# 1828 Roster of Fire Companies and Officers

The following pages are from the April 26, 1828 *Newbern Sentinel* listing a portion of the articles of a Constitution for the three fire companies plus Company 4 (volunteers).

### NEWBERN:

**SATURDAY, APRIL 26, 1828.**

#### SUPERIOR COURT.

The spring term of our Superior Court, his honor Judge Strange presiding, commenced its session on Monday last. The whole of the week was devoted to the trial of the various cases on the criminal docket: but no case of unusual interest was called, with the exception of that of Robert Spier, which was continued by the State on account of the absence of a material witness.

The speech of the Hon. Mr. Bryan on the Tariff, arrived too late for insertion in to-day's paper—It will be published in our next.

#### TOWN MEETING.

deference, suggest the propriety of instructing their representative to the next General Assembly, to effect a repeal of the act of 1820, so far as concerns the town of Newbern, limiting the number of men to be employed as firemen to sixty. Your committee would further recommend to this meeting, the organization of a Fire Company for each engine, to be commanded by a Captain and two Engineers; but as this measure cannot be accomplished and adopted, until the repeal of the act of 1820 is effected, they, in compliance with the resolution of this meeting, submit the following articles as a Constitution for the government of those who have voluntarily associated themselves, for the formation of a seperate and detached *Fire Company*.

*Article 1.* The company shall consist of at least twenty members, and all applicants for admission, hereafter, shall be proposed at a meeting preceding the election, and at that time be arrived at the age of fifteen years, and no person shall be elected or expelled, without the concurrence of two thirds of the members present.

*Article 2.* The stated meetings of the Company shall be held once in every month for the

#### FOR COMPANY—No. 1.

ROBERT PRIMROSE, *Captain,*
THOMAS CARNEY, 1st *Engineer,*
BENJAMIN CHENEY, 2nd do.
MATTHEW A OUTTEN, *Secretary.*
MOSES W. JARVIS, *Treasurer.*

#### FOR COMPANY—No. 2.

MARTIN STEVENSON, SR. *Captain,*
THOMAS SPARROW, 1st *Engineer.*
JOHN HARVEY. JR 2nd do.
OLIVER S. DEWEY, *Secretary.*
JEREMIAH N. ALLEN, *Treasurer.*

#### FOR COMPANY—No. 3.

HARDY B. LANE, *Captain,*
JAMES C. STEVENSON, 1st *Engineer,*
CLAUDIUS B. CHURCHILL, 2nd do.
MARTIN STEVENSON, JR *Secretary.*
JOSEPH OLIVER, *Treasurer.*

#### VOLUNTEER COMPANY.

WILLIAM HOLLISTER, *Captain,*
JOHN I. PASTEUR, 1st *Engineer,*
JOHN M. ROBERTS, 2nd do.
HENRY W JONES, *Secretary,*
JAMES W. BRYAN, *Treasurer.*

## TOWN MEETING.

According to previous arrangement, a Meeting of the citizens of this town was held in the Court-House on Monday evening last for the purpose of organizing Fire Companies. Col. JOHN I. PASTEUR was called to the Chair, and JAMES C. STEVENSON, Esq. appointed Secretary.

The following Report from the Board of Commissioners appointing three companies of twenty men each, was submitted to the Meeting and approved of:

### Office of Intendant of Police.

Present, the Hon. the Intendant of Police, and Commissioners.

The following named persons were selected from a list presented for that purpose, to be formed into three Fire Companies—who are hereby requested to organize the said Companies, choose their officers, form their by-laws, and report to the Commissioners as soon as may be for their approval.

present.

*Article 2.* The stated meetings of the Company shall be held once in every month for the purpose of exercising the Engine; and the members shall be notified thereof by the Secretary of the Company, and special meetings for the transaction of business, whenever six members shall request the Captain to call the same, and when business requires it, the Company may meet on their own adjournment.

*Article 3.* The Officers shall be a Captain, two Engineers, a Secretary, and Treasurer, to be elected immediately after the organization of the company, and to serve for one year from that time; and whenever a vacancy occurs, either by resignation or otherwise, the Company shall immediately elect to fill the vacancy.

*Article 4.* In all cases during the absence of the Captain of the Company, the first Engineer shall take his place; and during the absence of the Captain and first Engineer, the second Engineer shall fill the vacancy.

*Article 5.* The Captain, or in his absence, the first Engineer, or in the absence of both, the second Engineer, shall preside at all meetings, and use his utmost endeavours to have the Constitution and by-laws executed with energy and preserved inviolate. He shall call special meetings whenever six members shall request the same, put all motions to vote when seconded, and draw all orders on the Treasurer which are approved by a majority of the Company.

*Article 6.* The Secretary shall keep a book

## COMPANY No. 1.

Thomas Carney,
Charles G. Speight,
John S Morris,
George Bradford,
Robert Primrose,
George W. Dixon,
John Chadwick,
Henry Harvey,
Samuel B. Smith,
Nathaniel Smith,
John A. Crispin,
Major Cook,
M. W. Jarvis,
Alonzo T. Jerkins,
Benjamin Cheney,
Matthew A Outten,
John Hutchinson,
John G. Kincey,
E. C. O. Tinker,
Jacob Gooding.

## COMPANY No. 2.

W. M. Sears,
Enoch Alexander,
O. S Dewey,
James W. Smith,
Joseph F. Fowler,
Martin Stevenson, Sr.
Stephen Kincey,
Thomas Sparrow,
John Harvey, Jr.
Alfred Stanly,
Smith Sparrow,
James Riggs,
James Davis,
Alexander Mitchell,
H D Machen,
Lewis Bryan,
Jeremiah N. Allen,
W B. Wadsworth,
W G. Bryan,
E. J Fullshire.

## COMPANY No 3.

R. V. Orme,
James E Bettner,
Charles Slover,
William Babcock,
C. B. Churchill,
Joseph King,
James C Stevenson,
William B Toler,
H B Lane,
Zach. Slade,
Wm. Hindes,
Samuel G. Battle,
Alen Fitch,
Joseph W Jarvis,
Joseph Oliver,
John H Goldston,
Martin Stevenson, Jr.
Joseph F Anthony,
John A. Wilson,
John Siner.

Mr. J W. Bryan, from the Committee previously appointed for that purpose, made the following Report, which was unanimously adopted:

for fair and correct minutes of the proceedings of the Company, which shall be produced at every meeting for the transaction of business and be opened to the inspection of the members, during that time, and shall deliver them clear of incumbrances to his successor in office. He shall fill up and deliver to the messenger (who shall be employed by the Company) all notices at least twenty-four hours previous to stated, special, or adjourned meetings, and shall notify a new member, within a week after his election. He shall attest all orders drawn upon the Treasurer which are approved by the Company, and from time to time deliver to the Treasurer a list of the members who have incurred any fines, either by absence or otherwise, for which purpose he shall call the roll in thirty minutes after the time of meeting specified in the notice, and after a fire as soon as the Engine is housed, and all necessary duty done, and in case of his absence, he shall cause to be kept in the Engine House, a list of the members' names, to be called and noted by any other officer present.

*Article* 7. The Treasurer shall keep a fair and true account of all monies received and paid by him on account of the company—his book shall be produced at every meeting, and be opened to the inspection of the members—he shall pay no orders unless signed by the Captain and attested by the Secretary—he shall regularly charge all fines which the members incur, and shall notify each member, in writing, of the amount of his fines, within six months after the first shall become due; and previous to the election of officers, he shall deliver to the Captain, a list of the members so notified, who are six months in arrears to the Company, that their votes may be rejected.

*Article* 8. It shall be the duty of the Captain, or in his absence, the Engineers, immediately on the alarm of the fire, to repair to the Engine

# Appendix G

# Fire Station Locations

The earliest known location for a fire engine house was in 1829 when a garage was built for a new hand pumper on George Street near the residence of John Stanly (307 George Street).

The Neuse Engine Co. was in the 200 block of Craven Street in the1850s. Lady Washington was on Craven Street near the *North Carolina Times* office 1862-1865.

### New Bern Steam Fire Engine Co., aka Palmer Engine (1865), Button Co. (1884-Pres.)

The Palmer Engine Company No. 1 (New Bern Steam Engine Co.) which formed in early 1865 had a firehouse on Craven Street next door to the *New Berne Times* building. In March 1866 there was a reference to the firehouse being the Pell house building when they extended the building to accommodate a hook and ladder. By June 1871, they had moved into a new firehouse in the 300 block of Broad Street. between Craven and Middle Street.

(Left) New Bern Steam Engine firehouse in the 300 block of Broad Street between Craven and Middle Street, north side. *New Bern Firemen's Museum Collection.*

1887 NBSFE at 41 Middle Street. From 1895 to 1898 the engine company was at City Hall.

The New Bern Steam Engine Company moved into a building on the northeast corner of Hancock and Broad Street owned by past chief engineer Barrington in early 1898. The lease was for 5 years. (Jan. 8, 1898 *The Daily Journal*)

Button Company at City Hall 1904-1913, on Craven Street between South Front and Pollock Street (east side) in 1913.

Relocated to the new Broad Street station 1928-1999.

## Atlantic Company
Atlantic Company was next to the police station in 1869

In 1883 the Atlantic Fire Company was located next to the Daily Journal newspaper on Middle Street. By 1885 they were in the Old City Hall at 228 Craven Street.

Atlantic at City Hall, Craven St. 1904-1913, relocated to 405 Broad Street. 1913-1928.

April 27, 1915...The Atlantics' new American Lafrance engine was kept at their building on Broad Street (owned by T.A. Green). Changes were made to the building including adding a brass sliding pole from the third to first floor and new sleeping quarters. (Apr 27, 1915 *New Bern Weekly Journal*)

Moved to the new Broad Street station 1928-1999.

## Reliance Company
Reliance Company was on Metcalf Street in 1869...George Street. in the 1870s and on Broad Street in 1890.

## Excelsiors
The Excelsior Fire Company house was the Lane building, adjoining the Holden House on Middle Street. Around 1885 the Excelsiors were co-located with the Mechanics Hook & Ladder in the former Atlantic Steam Engine Company.

## Rough & Ready and Mechanics Hook and Ladder
The Chief recommended that a building be erected to the rear of the city's buildings for the use of the Rough and Ready and Mechanics Hook and Ladder companies. (*The Daily Journal* May 10, 1890)

In 1895, a brick building opposite J.J. Disosway & Co. underwent changes to adapt the structure for the Rough and Ready Hook & Ladder Co. and their new hook and ladder truck. It would also house a hose cart and horse as well as a pair of mules to haul the hook and ladder. There would be sleeping quarters for the drivers. (Oct. 3, 1895 *The Daily Journal*) By April 1898, they were located on Cypress Street near the corner of National Avenue opposite the New Bern Tobacco warehouse.

**City Hall on Craven St., home to both the New Bern Steam and Atlantic companies over the years.** *Photo by Andrew Bartholf*

## Fourth Ward Hose
Fourth Ward at 141 Broad Street between Fleet and Bern Street (South side)

## Fourth Ward (Black)
On Pasteur Street just above the railroad station.

## Fifth Ward Hose
Fifth Ward firehouse was on Norwood Street near Queen at McCarthy's cart-house.

## Sixth Ward Hose
Sixth Ward was on the corner of George and Cypress Street (East side) on the edge of the

Cedar Grove cemetery.

## **Riverside Hose**
Riverside near National Avenue and Avenue A in 1911…moved to the corner of George and Cypress Street (east side) in 1912 (possibly into the old Sixth Ward firehouse).

**Home to the Atlantic Company, 405 Broad St., 1913-1928** *Photo by Andrew Bartholf*

Location of Fourth Ward on Broad St., near the current location of the Country Biscuit.  *Photo by Andrew Bartholf*

Location of Sixth Ward Hose Company. now part of cemetery.  *Photo by Andrew Bartholf*

**Broad Street Station 1928-1999. Housed both the Atlantic and Button companies. Note bear protruding from building near the American flag.** *Photo by Andrew Bartholf*

**Bear on front of fire station. Originally, this and 2 other bears were mounted on the old City Hall** *Photo by Andrew Bartholf*

**Station 2, 1620 Totten Drive, 1951-2000. Located behind the current Station 1.** *Photo by Andrew Bartholf*

**Station 2 in 1955.** *Courtesy NCSFA*

**Station 3 1700 National Ave, 1955-2004**  *Photo by Andrew Bartholf*

**Station 3 in 1955.**  *Courtesy NCSFA*

**Station 3 Elizabeth Ave. (2000-Present). Known as Station 4 (1976-2000)** *Photo by Andrew Bartholf*

Station 1 Neuse Blvd. 1999-Present      *Photo by Andrew Bartholf*

**Station 2  Thurman Road   (2002-Present)**                                                                                   *Photo by Author*

# Appendix H

# Steam & Motorized Apparatus

This appendix contains a list of all steam and motorized apparatus. Missing from this section are details about the hand pumpers, hose wagons and carriages, hook & ladder trucks, both horse and hand-drawn, of which we have very little information. In addition, a tradition naming fire equipment after important long-time members and mayors in the city began with the Silsby steamer. Elijah Ellis was a member of the Atlantic Company who donated the two horses to pull the steamer. The Atlantics would continue to do this while the New Bern Steam Company did not. Eventually all new vehicles would carry the name of the mayor at the time of delivery.

**Amoskeag Steamer 550 GPM Third Size s/n 127 delivered 4/25/1865**  *Courtesy State Archives of North Carolina*

**1879 Silsby 600 GPM Steamer 4th Size "Elijah Ellis"  s/n 604**  *Photo by Andrew Bartholf*

**1884 Button 500 GPM Steamer Fourth Size  s/n 155**  *Photo by Andrew Bartholf*

1914 American LaFrance Type 12 750 GPM Rotary Gear Chemical Engine  s/n 689          *Albert Brinson Jr. Collection*

American LaFrance Type 12 750 GPM s/n 812 "William Ellis" delivered 4/16/1915   *Ernest C. Richardson III Collection*

Ford Model AA hose wagon, unknown builder.   *Courtesy NCSFA.*

1927 Seagrave City Service 1000 GPM  "Albert H. Bangert"  s/n 49750

*Photo by Andrew Bartholf*

**1933 American LaFrance 285 1000 GPM "Leon C. Scott" s/n 7043 shipped 10/31/1934**   *Courtesy of New Bern Fire Rescue; Photo by Henry Watson*

**1936 International W.S. Darley, 500 GPM "Edgar B. Elliott"**   *Courtesy NCSFA*

1945 American LaFrance B-675CO 750 GPM s/n L-2327 "L.C. Lawrence" shipped 1/7/1946  *Courtesy NCSFA*

1951 Dodge John Bean -Craven County, high pressure pump only, s/n 601 Delivered 7/22/1951.  *Courtesy*

**1952 GMC Oren Roanoke 500 GPM    "George H. Roberts"**    *Courtesy NCSFA*

**GMC John Bean 750 GPM "Mack L. Lupton" s/n 838 delivered Oct. 19, 1954**    *Courtesy NCSFA*

1963 Seagrave 85' Ladder delivered 1/19/1964   "Dr. Dale T. Millns"   *Courtesy of New Bern Fire Rescue; Photo by Henry Watson*

**Delivered February, 1964 Seagrave 1000 GPM "Mack L. Lupton"** *Courtesy of New Bern Fire Rescue; Photo by Henry Watson*

**1969 Ford Ward LaFrance 1000 GPM "Cecil King"** *Courtesy of New Bern Fire Rescue; Photo by Henry Watson*

**1973 Ford Ward LaFrance 1000 GPM "Ethridge H. Ricks"**  *Courtesy of New Bern Fire Rescue; Photo by Henry Watson*

**1978 Ford Pierce 1000 GPM "Charles H. Kimbrell"**  *Courtesy of New Bern Fire Rescue; Photo by Henry Watson*

**Refurbished 1978 Ford**  *Courtesy of New Bern Fire Rescue; Photo by Henry Watson*

**1983 Ford Quality 1000 GPM "Paul M. Cox"**  *Courtesy of New Bern Fire Rescue; Photo by Henry Watson*

**1984 Chevrolet Step-Van "Leander B. Morgan"** *Courtesy of New Bern Fire Rescue; Photo by Henry Watson*

**1985 Ford American LaFrance 1000 GPM "Paul M. Cox"** *Courtesy of New Bern Fire Rescue; Photo by Henry Watson*

1987 Ford Quality 1000 GPM "Ella Bengel"  *Photo by Andrew Bartholf*

1999 Sutphen 100'+ Tower HS-3400  "Tom Bayliss"  *Courtesy of New Bern Fire Rescue; Photo by Henry Watson*

# Current Apparatus

**1992 Sutphen 1500 GPM Engine   HS-2755   "Leander B. Morgan"**               *Photo by Author*

1993	International Rescue  "Leander B. Morgan"	*Photo by Author*

2002 Sutphen 1500 GPM   HS-3653   "Tom Bayliss"   *Courtesy of New Bern Fire Rescue; Photo by Henry Watson*

2007 Sutphen Quint s/n HS-4137, 1500 GPM Quint     "Tom Bayliss"     *Photo by Andrew Bartholf*

2014 Sutphen Quint s/n HS-54671500 GPM     "Lee W. Bettis Jr."     Photo by Author

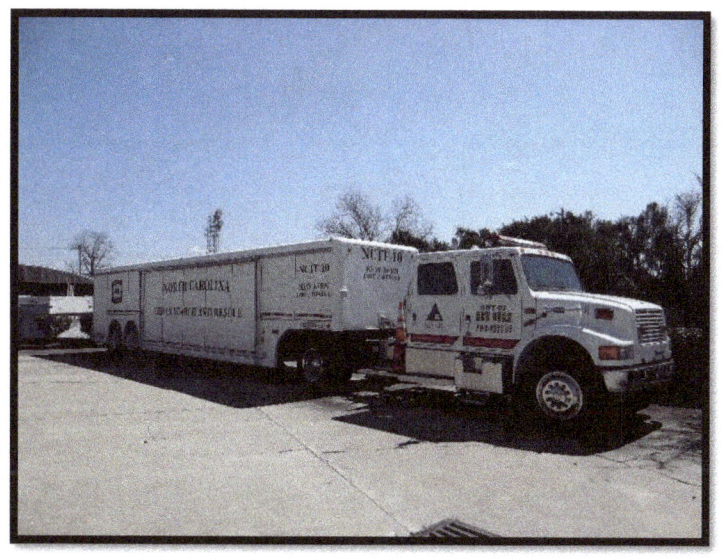

North Carolina Task Force 10 Urban Search & Rescue  Photo *by Andrew Bartholf*

2020 Sutphen 100+ Tower s/n HS-6610, 1500 GPM, 300 Gallons water.    "Dana Outlaw"    *Picture by Andrew Bartholf*

**2020 Sutphen Engine s/n HS-6611, 1500 GPM, 750 Gallons Water   "Dana Outlaw"   *Photo by Andrew Bartholf***

**1998 Sutphen 1500 GPM   HS-366  "Tom Bayliss"  Courtesy of New Bern Fire  *Photo by Henry Watson***

# Appendix I

# Notification of Fire

In the early days, the church bell was sounded upon learning of a fire in the city. Word of mouth was the only way to learn of the location of the fire once the firemen assembled. This often led to a delay in response due to confusion about the location. Eventually enough smoke would fill the sky making the location easily identifiable, but often too late to save the structure.

A night watch was established by late in the 1700s in which citizens took turns patrolling the streets overnight. The Christ Church bell would be rung at 9 pm to announce the beginning of the watch. Their duty was to spot fires and criminal activity. When they spotted a fire, one of the members of the watch would respond to the church to ring the bell, while other members would notify residents near the fire of the danger and ask them to assist in quelling the fire.

The first fire alarm bell was installed on top of a two-story frame building that served as the city hall near the location of the current Craven County courthouse. It was later moved to the new city hall on Craven Street once occupied by a tobacco company. Another bell was located on a tower at Five Points.

**Fire bell originally at the City Hall.** Photo by Andrew Bartholf

Bell on Firemen's Memorial was located at Five Points.                Photo by Andrew Bartholf

December 26, 1867...New Bern Steam Fire granted approval for a bell tower.

At the urging of Chief Engineer Brinson, the fire bell was moved to the police station in June 1869.

Ten fire alarm boxes were installed on the streets of the city around the same time as a water system was completed with fire hydrants in 1893. The fire alarm bells were tied into the system. When a fire box was activated (pulled), the bells within the city would tap out the box number. Indicators in the stations would also show the box number.

The lumber companies in the city had steam whistles to alert plant employees and the citizens of fires at the plants.

Chief W.D. Barrington announced the following Water Works fire alarm signals in July 1894: 1 tap, keep stand-pipe pressure up; 5 taps, pump direct through main; 2 taps, shut off direct pressure and pump in stand-pipe; 3 taps, fire out. (July 29, 1894 *The Daily Journal*)

There were problems with the early box alarm system. As an example, a house fire on Bern street on December 1, 1902 highlighted the problems. Two attempts were made to turn in the alarm from boxes 54 and 55. The result was the bell struck only once. The system had been overhauled only three months earlier. (Dec. 2, 1902 *New Berne Weekly Journal*)

By 1904, fire alarm bells were located at City Hall, A & N.C. Railroad Depot and at Five Points.

More problems with the fire alarm system in March 1906. An attempt to send an alarm at the corner of George and Cypress Streets failed to sound. Someone had to run to the next box at New and George to sound the alarm. (March 6, 1906 *New Berne Weekly Journal*)

February 3, 1909.... A General alarm will be 7 taps calling for high pressure and the entire department, a Third alarm calls for the Fifth Ward hose wagon to the downtown district (it answers no alarm east of George St and south of Queen St). The All Out notification is 3 taps. (Feb. 4, 1909 *The New Bern Sun*)

The number of box alarm locations changed over the years. From 1903 through 1913 there were 20 boxes.

Jan. 1914...Riverside Hose Co petitions the city for an indicator (for fire alarms). Referred to Fire Dept Committee for action (Jan. 7, 1914 *The Daily Journal*)

**Indicator Alarms-displays box alarm**  *Photos by Andrew Bartholf*

With 14 of the 20 fire alarm boxes out of service in early 1914, a new system was installed which included 15 "imaginary stations" (box alarm locations). At city hall there was an electronic map of the city with apertures at various points allowing for the installation of a plug. If someone telephoned in an alarm of fire to city hall, the official answering the phone could insert a plug into the aperture nearest to the fire location. This would cause the alarm to be triggered from the closest alarm box. This was the first installation of its kind in the state. In addition, instead of having all alarm boxes on just one circuit, two circuits were installed. This would prevent a complete outage of the alarm system as happened in January 1914. (Feb. 18, 1914 *The Daily Journal*)

The Fire Alarm System was nearing completion in August 1914. A switchboard and storage batteries were put in place. All new wiring was strung to the fire alarm boxes. With the overhaul of the system, there were 31 boxes. (Aug. 7, 1914 *The Daily Journal*)

A new fire whistle was installed on top of the water and light plant sometime during 1916.

June 1920...Fire Alarm bell in the belfry of the municipal building, in use for many years is cracked and silent. A new bell was ordered. (June 11, 1920 *New Bern Sun Journal*)

March 23, 1948...Chief T.I. Davis requested a fire alarm whistle. Granted.

June 1950... New Gamewell fire alarm system purchased for $18,261.89. The purchase included the installation of 110 box alarms.

Sep. 7, 1954....Bids for radio equipment for the fire trucks. Motorola $5036.63 and GE $5040.00. Bid awarded to Motorola.

Nov. 6, 1956....only 36 of 110 fire alarm boxes installed.

January 2, 1959...Motorola awarded a contract for base station and 20 home alerting monitors for volunteers. The department was on low band frequencies at this point in time.

April-May 1965...dispatching system installed at New Bern Broad St station.

In February 1987 Station Chief Aster recommended the removal of the fire alarm boxes as they had become unreliable. The boxes were removed and sold by the end of the year.

The department moved from low band frequencies to 800 MHz upon the opening of the new Station 1 in 1999.

# Fire Alarm Box Locations

### New Bern Fire Alarm.

No. 1-2 Foot of Craven street.
" 1-4 Cor. South Ft. and East Ft. streets.
" 1-5 Blades Mill, King street.
" 1-6 Ice Factory, Griffith street.
" 1-7 Blades Mill, Griffith street.
" 2-4 Cor. South Ft. and Middle street.
" 2-5 Cor. Hancock and Broad street.
" 2-6 Cor Johnson and Middle streets
" 3-2 Cor George and Pollock streets
" 3-4 Cor. George and New streets.
" 3-5 Cor George and Cypress streets
" 4-2 Elm City Mills.
" 4-7 Cor. New S. Ft. and Spring streets.
" 4-8 Cor. Broad and Bern streets.
" 5-1 Cor. Norwood and Crooked streets.
" 5-2 Five Points.
" 5-3 Cor. Elm and Ash streets.
" 5-4 Cor. West and Cedar streets.
" 5-5 Cor. Main street and Pavi Avenue.
" 6 2 Pine Lumber Company.

Source: May 7, 1903 *The Daily Journal*

### LOCATION OF FIRE ALARM BOXES.

12, Foot Craven street.
14, S. Front, corner E. Front.
15, Neuse Lumber Co., King street
16, Ice Factory, Griffith street.
17, Congdon Mill, Griffith street.
24, S. Front, corner Middle.
25, Hancock, corner Broad.
26, Johnson, corner Middle.
32, George, corner Pollock.
34, George, corner New.
35, George, corner Cypress.
42, Elm City Lumber Co.
47, New S. Front street, corner Spring.
48 Broad, corner Burn.
51 McCarthy's store.
52, Five Points.
53 Elm, corner Ashe.
54, West, corner Cidar.
55, Main, corner Pavic avenue.
62, Pine Lumber Co.

Aug. 27, 1913 *The Daily Journal*

## LOCATION FIRE ALARM BOXES NEW BERN, N. C.

BOX NO.
- 12 South Front and East Front Sts.
- 13 Broad and East Front Sts.
- 14 South Front and Middle
- 15 Pollock and Middle.
- 16 Broad and Hancock.
- 17 Johnson and Middle.
- (18) New and Craven.
- (23) South Front and Metcalf.
- 24 Pollock and George.
- 25 South Front and Burn.
- (27) Pollock and Fleet.
- (28) South Front and Jones.
- (29) South Front and Bryan.
- (31) Water and Light Plant
- 32 Pollock and Queen
- 34 Broad and Burn.
- 35 New and George.
- (36) Johnson and Metcalf.
- 42 Broad and Queen.
- (45) Broad and Chapman.
- 47 Elm and Ash.
- 48 Cedar and West.
- 51 King and East Front
- 52 Griffith Street (Ice Factory)
- 53 Cypress and George.
- 54 Main and Murray.
- 55 Crescent and Griffith.
- (56) Pine and Burn.
- (61) National Ave. and Ave. A.
- 62 Griffith and Ave. C. (John L. Roper Lumber Company)
- (63) National Ave. and Ave. C.

NOTE: Until the system can be

Source: March 21, 1914 *The Daily Journal*

---

**P. A. DIXON** PHONE 103. 69½ BROAD STREET.
**Plumbing and Heating Contractor**

NEW BERN, N C (1916-17) DIRECTORY

## DIRECTORY OF
## Miscellaneous Information

*Giving Information Regarding City and County Governments, Churches, Fraternal Orders, Societies, Etc.*

Compiled by CHAS. S. GARDINER

### CITY GOVERNMENT
- City Hall—51 Craven
- Mayor—A H Bangert
- City Clerk—F T Patterson
- City Tax Collector—J J Tolson
- City Treasurer—D M Roberts
- City Engineer—R R Eagle
- City Attorney—R A Nunn
- Post Physician—J F Patterson
- Supt Water Works & Electric Light Plant—H H Hodges
- Collector Water and Light Dept—F M Scott

### Board of Alderman
- First Ward—Wm Ellis, C H Hall
- Second Ward—W B Blades, S H Scott
- Third Ward—A T Dill, J B Dawson
- Fourth Ward—T F McCarthy, J C Brinson
- Fifth Ward—R J Disosway, John Crabtree

### Fire Department
- Chief—Samuel Coward
- Atlantic Steam Fire Engine Co No 1—Broad nr Middle, B F Williams, chf engr; R L Pitman asst engr
- Button Steam Fire Engine Co No 1—45 Craven, B F Williams chf engr; Zack Styron asst engr

### Fire Alarm Boxes
Box No
- 12—South and East Front
- 13—Broad and East Front
- 14—South Front and Middle
- 15—Pollock and Middle
- 16—Broad and Hancock
- 17—Johnson and Middle
- 18—New and Craven
- 23—South Front and Metcalf
- 24—Pollock and George
- 25—South Front and Burn
- 27—Pollock and Fleet
- 28—South Front and Jones
- 29—South Front and Bryan
- 31—Water and Light Plant
- 32—Pollock and Queen
- 34—Broad and Burn
- 35—New and George
- 36—Johnson and Metcalf
- 42—Broad and Queen
- 45—Broad and Chapman
- 47—Elm and Ash
- 48—Cedar and West
- 51—King and East Front
- 52—Griffith Street
- 53—Cypress and George
- 54—Main and Murry
- 55—Crescent and Griffith
- 56—Pine and Burn
- 61—National and Avenue A
- 62—Griffith and Avenue C
- 63—National and Avenue C

**New Bern Cotton Oil & Fertilizer Mills**
NEW BERN, N. C.
Buyers of Cotton Seed and Manufacturers of Cotton Seed Products.

Source: 1916-17 New Bern Business Directory

## LOCATION OF FIRE ALARM BOXES
### For New Bern, N. C.

7—Emergency
8—Stand By
13—Ave. A & Windley St. Barbour Boat Works
16—Episcopal Church
17—Montgomery Ward
18—Hospital
19—Guardian Care
21—Nichols
22—New Bern Academy
25—Judge Gaston House
26—Barbour Boat Works
27—Social Service (Broad & George)
29—Tryon Palace
32—McDaniel Rest Home
35—New Bern Towers
38—Mission Rest Home
39—Ramada Inn
44—Out of Town

### ZONE 1
111—Broad & Hancock
112—Broad & Middle
113—Broad & Craven
114—Broad & East Front
115—Craven & Pollock
116—Middle & Pollock
117—Middle & Tryon Palace Dr.
118—East Front & Tryon Palace Dr.
121—Central School
122—Johnson & Middle New Library
123—East Front & Linden St.
124—East Front & King
125—Craven & New
126—Metcalf & Tryon Palace Dr.
127—Johnson & Metcalf
128—George & New
129—George & Pollock
131—Fleet & Tryon Palace Dr.
132—Bern & Broad
133—Fleet & Pollock
134—Jones & New South Front
135—Bryant & New South Front
136—Pembroke Rd. & Rhem
137—Hancock & Queen
138—Bern & Queen
139—Broad & Queen
141—Pollock & Queen
142—First & Queen
143—First & Pollock
144—Rhem Ave. & Third
145—Park Ave. & Third
146—Fourth & Spencer Ave.
147—Fifth & Park Ave.
148—Fifth & Rhem Ave.
149—Sixth & Spencer Ave.
151—Eighth & Spencer Ave.
152—Queen Anne Lane & Trent Blvd.
153—Ft. Totten Dr. & Lucerne Way
154—Chattawka Lane & Tryon Rd.
155—Lucerne Way & Tryon Rd.
156—Colonial Place
157—DeGraffenfied Ave. & Tryon Rd.
158—Cleveland & Jefferson Ave.
159—Franklin Ave. & Jackson
161—Stewart Blvd. & Trent Blvd.
162—Center Ave. & Eighth
163—Grace Ave. & Ninth
164—Henderson Ave. & Ninth
165—Griffin Ave. & Simmons
166—Center Ave. & Simmons
167—Henderson Ave. & Forest
168—Simmons & Trent Blvd.
169—Ninth & Trent Blvd.

### ZONE 2
211—North Craven (Ice Plant)
212—Crescent & North Craven
213—Avenue A & North Craven
214—Avenue C & North Craven
224—Avenue B & North Pasteur
225—Avenue D & North Pasteur
232—Cypress & George
233—Avenue A & National Ave.
234—Avenue C & National Ave.
235—North Ave. & National Ave.
236—Court & National Ave.
237—River Dr.
244—Blades Ave. & Cutler
245—National Court Dr. & Cutler
251—Asheville & Contentnea Ave.
252—Contentnea Ave. & Edenton
253—Trent Ave. & Wilmington
254—Edenton & Neuse Ave.
255—Fayetteville & Neuse Ave.
256—Asheville & Neuse Ave.
291—Hatteras Yacht

### ZONE 3
311—Cedar & West
312—Elm & Rountree
313—Green & Cedar
314—Cedar & First Ave.
315—Broad & Chapman
317—Elm & Second Ave.
318—Cedar & Third Ave.
321—Bern & Main
322—Main & Murray
323—Green & Main
324—Main & Garden St.
325—Cypress & West
326—Bloomfield & North
327—Eubanks & North
328—F & K
331—Biddle & Harrison
332—Myrtle Ave. & William
333—Garden & Williams
334—Garden & Goldsboro
335—Beaufort & Garden
336—Lark & Lincoln
337—Carver & Cobb
338—J. T. Barber School
339—Washington & Hazel

### ZONE 4
411—Broad & Gaston Blvd.
412—Ft. Totten Ave. & McArthur Ave.
413—Devers Ave. & Queen Anne Lane
414—Neuse Blvd. & Queen Anne Lane
415—Chattawka Lane & Colonial Way
416—Clark Ave. & Neuse Blvd.
417—DeGraffenried Ave. & Neuse Blvd.
418—Williams & West Memorial Home
419—Helen Ave. & Neuse Blvd.
421—Helen Ave. & Waters
422—Hazel Ave. & Waters
423—Neuse Blvd. & Simmons
424—Forest Hills
425—Dogwood Ave. & Laurel St.
426—Phillips Ave. & Neuse Blvd.
427—High & Phillips Ave.
428—Benfield Dr. & Edgewood
429—Neuse Blvd. & Benfield Dr.
431—Neuse Blvd. & Cherry Tree. Dr.
432—Cherry Tree Dr.
433—Neuse Blvd. & Longview Dr.
434—Elizabeth Ave. & Longview Dr.
435—Elizabeth Ave. & Cherry Lane
436—Educational Dr. & Simmons
437—Trent Park School
438—No. Grace Ave. & Woodland Ave.
439—Pine Tree Dr. & Woodland Ave.
441—Simmons & Woodland Ave.
442—Meadows & Tatum Dr.
443—New Bern High School
444—High School Dr. & Meadows
445—Newton Dr. & Tatum Dr.
446—Meadows & Simmons
447—High School Dr. & Simmons
448—Bray & High
451—Berne Square
453—South Square

### ZONE 5
515—Mammoth Mart
516—Holiday City
517—Elizabeth Ave. & So. Glenburnie Dr.
518—Plymouth Dr. & Roanoke Ave.
519—Colony Dr. & Plymouth Dr.
521—Neuse Blvd. & So. Glenburnie Rd.
522—Craven Community College
524—Yarmouth Rd.
531—Colony Estate
532—Racetrack Rd. & Neuse Blvd.
533—Neuse Blvd. & Pinecrest Ave.
534—Pinecrest Ave. & Powell St.
535—Karen St. & Midyette Ave.
536—Neuse Blvd. & Midyette Ave.
551—Crown Moving and Storage
554—Kensington Park Apts.
555—Stanley Tool
556—Texfi

### ZONE 6
611—Modern Moving and Storage
612—New Bern Moving and Storage
613—McCauley Bro. Moving

### CODES:
Code 1—False Alarm
Code 2—Small Fire
Code 3—Working Fire
Code 4—Out On Arriving or Fire Extinguished
Code 5—
Code 6—Unnecessary

1982

1982 Fire Alarm Locations

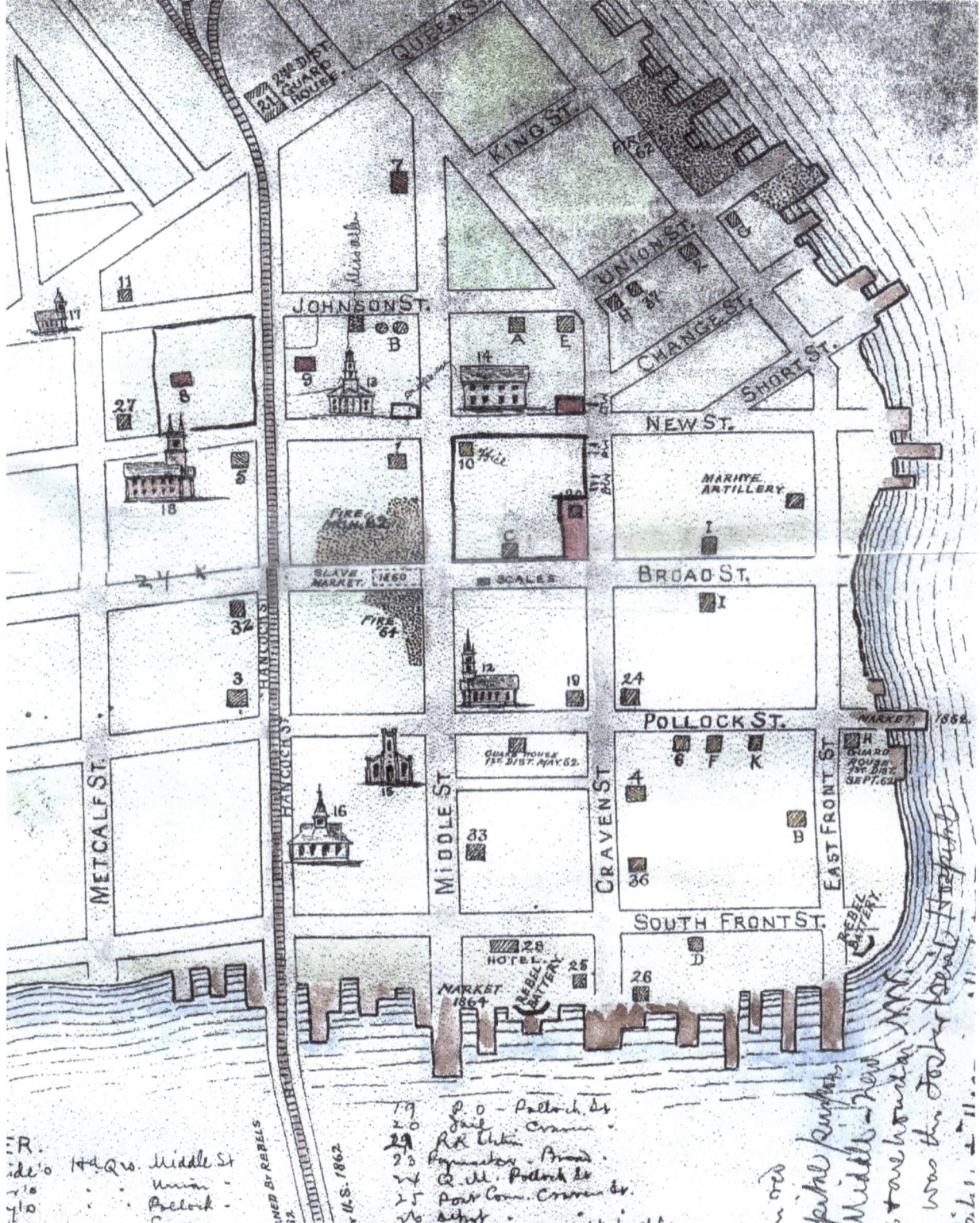

**Fires set by Confederates upon feeing the city in 1862. Also note the fire on the corner of Middle and Broad St. in 1864 which led to the purchase of New Bern's first steamer by the military. Of interest is the slave market on Broad St near Middle which was present around 1860.**

Courtesy John B. Green III

## About the Author

Dan was in the volunteer fire service for 45 years serving in several departments in New York State, but also North Carolina and West Virginia. He held positions of Chief, Assistant Chief, Captain and Lieutenant and was certified as a Level II Firefighter and Hazmat Technician. He wrote articles for *Fire Chief, Firehouse* and *Engine! Engine!* (official publication of the Society for the Preservation and Appreciation of Antique Motorized Fire Apparatus in America- SPAAMFAA) magazines.

He was employed as a meteorologist with the National Weather Service for 35 years serving in offices in Buffalo, Albany, Syracuse, Newport (NC), and Charleston (WV).

Dan holds a Bachelor of Science Degree in Meteorology from the State University of New York at Oneonta and a Masters Degree in Public Administration and Emergency Management from Jacksonville State University.

www.ingramcontent.com/pod-product-compliance
Lightning Source LLC
Chambersburg PA
CBHW061747290426
44108CB00028B/2919